Dominic Salles still lives in Swindon, with his workaholic wife Deirdre. His jiu-jitsu-loving ex-engineer son, Harry, has moved to Shoreditch and lives on the site of Shakespeare's first theatre. Destiny. For those of you who remember Bob, he is now an ex-dog.

His daughter Jess is educating students in Wales because, now Brexit is done, Brussels isn't stepping in to help the Welsh any more. She is learning to surf. He spent three months in Andorra this year, learning to snowboard. He is not as cool as he thinks.

His sister Jacey is famous for her Spanish accent, on your TV screens, and is also filming in Wales. She would be hilarious in her own YouTube channel. His 2006 Prius has just died and been rein*car*nated (who writes these puns?) as a 2019 Prius.

His YouTube channel, Mr Salles Teaches English, has reached 100,000 subscribers, about which he is childishly excited. 30% of his viewers said they improved by at least 3 grades in 2022.

Other Grade 9 Guides by Mr Salles

Language

The Mr Salles Guide to **100% at AQA GCSE English Language**
The Mr Salles Guide to **Awesome Story Writing**
The Mr Salles Quick Guide to **Awesome Description**
The Mr Salles **Ultimate Guide to Description**
The Mr Salles Quick Guide to **Grammar, Punctuation and Spelling**
The Mr Salles Ultimate Guide to **Persuasive Writing**
The Mr Salles Guide to **100% in AQA GCSE English Language Paper 1 Question 2**
The Mr Salles Guide to **100% in AQA GCSE English Language Paper 1 Question 3**
The Mr Salles Guide to **100% in AQA GCSE English Language Paper 1 Question 4**
The Mr Salles Guide to **100% in AQA GCSE English Language Paper 1 Question 5**

Literature
The Mr Salles Guide to **GCSE English Literature**
Study Guide Mr Salles Analyses **Jekyll and Hyde**
The Mr Salles Ultimate Guide to **Macbeth**
The Mr Salles Guide to **An Inspector Calls**
The Mr Salles Ultimate Guide to **A Christmas Carol**
The Mr Salles Ultimate Guide to **Romeo and Juliet**
Mr Salles **Power and Conflict** Top Grade Essay Guide (AQA Anthology): 11 Grade 9 Exam Essays!

Introduction

This guide is built round such a simple idea, that I'm shocked I never thought of it before.

The best way to understand exam answers is to read exam answers!

I want my readers to have a huge range of exam answers to past questions. You will get at least 24 answers, all marked to show you the full range of the mark scheme.

And I also give you my commentary for each one as to why the marks were awarded.

In real life, most of these answers would be full of spelling and punctuation errors. But I've made sure that the spelling and punctuation is correct, so you can focus precisely on the exam skills of each question.

I've also rewritten each answer so that they actually make sense, and so that the students who wrote them wouldn't recognise them. I've changed most words, so 'green' becomes 'red', 'he' becomes 'she', 'fast' becomes 'quick' etc. It means the skills, sentences, detail, type of vocabulary, alliteration, metaphor, simile, personification etc is exactly the same as the actual students used, while nearly all the individual words are changed.

How to Use This Guide

All the answers are based on actual exam papers, which you can download from the AQA website. For copyright reasons, I can't give you the actual questions.

However, the guide will work brilliantly on its own, without the exam papers if you prefer.

1. Any time you sit any exam question, put your answer alongside this guide. Ask yourself, "which answer in the guide looks most like my answer?"

2. This will give you a very good guide as to what mark your answer would get.

3. Then read my commentary underneath.

4. This will tell you the sorts of things you are probably doing wrong.

5. Now, read the answers that scored more than this. Build up an idea of what gets more marks. This is even more valuable than my examiner's comments. But, you should read those too, because they teach you everything you need to know.

6. Now, write your answer again, without looking at the guide. This is the **only** way for you to work out if your exam skills are improving. If you answer a **different** question from a different paper, you won't know if you miss marks because you haven't understood the text properly, or because of a lack of exam technique.

7. **After** you have practised exam technique a couple of times, then you should try a **new** exam paper. This will measure how much improvement you have actually made, and tell you what mark you are likely to get if you took the GCSE now.

Introduction to Question 5

The Problem with Descriptive Writing

When AQA show teachers top grade writing, it is nearly always a *story*, not a description.

I think this is because they realise the description question is not real writing. Real authors don't write 400-600 word descriptions. But they do write chapters and stories, where description forms a *natural and helpful way to understand the characters or setting*. Description therefore has to have a purpose, *it is **never** just to prove to the reader that you know lots of descriptive writing skills!*

So, with the description question, AQA realise that they have created a monster, which is out of control. It's out of control because most schools tell you to do the description rather than the story. And, as you will see in this guide, most of the descriptions are poor.

AQA's solution is to show teachers quite a few stories, in the hope that students will be taught story writing.

They could have published a guide of great short stories, but they are probably scared stiff that students would simply copy them.

The Problem with Story Writing

But you'll also see some of the problems with writing a story. Some of the stories don't quite get the very top marks, because the student hasn't used enough simile, metaphor or personification. In other words, doing what real writers do can stop you getting the top grade. Because real writers don't cram their stories with these techniques. They just use them when it helps.

So, I've also included some stories that scored 40/40, full marks, 100% as marked by senior examiners.

Teachers, on the other hand, can see all the ways stories go wrong:

1. Poor writers keep swapping between past and present tense.
2. Good writers tend to forget to use similes, metaphors and personifications.
3. All writers struggle to think of a fitting ending to a story, because they are under exam pressure. Endings can be hard.

So, faced with a choice of teaching something students can easily mess up, teachers opt for the easier route. They also want to increase the chances that most students won't mess up.

Teachers live in fear. If you are worried about taking 10 GCSEs, I get it. But a teacher can have 30 students in a class, which is 30 results to worry about. Some will have two GCSE classes. So many teachers are 3 to 6 times more scared than you are. I wish I were joking.

So I understand why teachers would train you to do the description question, and not the story. But, while I understand this fear, I don't give in to it. I want all my students to write stories. If you want to learn, there are many here to inspire you. But, if you only want to learn to describe, you can do that here too.

Just as usefully, you will find all the ways that students lose marks. Understand all their mistakes, so you can avoid them.

Once you've read through this guide, you will understand exactly how to get the marks you deserve.

Then it is just a matter of practice and stealing ideas.

What is Plagiarism?

When you copy something word for word. This is the equivalent of stealing, and will lead to you getting really low marks if the examiner catches you. Now that I have over 100,000 subscribers on YouTube, there is a good chance that your examiner will have come across this guide. Also, regardless, don't steal, respect your parents, don't do drugs, just say no, etc. And be kind. Especially to people, not just to dogs.

What Isn't Plagiarism?

1. You can reproduce any of the plots, settings or characters.
2. You can repeat as many of the individual words as you like.
3. You can memorise whole sentence structures and patterns.
4. What you can't do is write down more than 2-3 words in a phrase which are exactly the same as in this book.
5. However, you can adapt them as much as you like. That is how I wrote this guide. I rewrote students' real answers. I kept their ideas and their structure for each sentence. I just changed 99% of the words. Once you've done this, you can use whatever you like.

What do I do When I Practise Question 5?

I write from scratch, because I want to be a good writer. I love English, reading, and writing. So I want to write a story I can be proud of.

But I understand that some of you just want to pass the exam. So, steal, don't plagiarise.

(N.b. About 50% of exam answers involve the student writing about blood, death, or murder. You will notice none of that happens in this guide!)

What have you learned?

_____

_____

_____

_____

_____

_____

_____

_____

_____

_____

The Mr Salles Method

I've written lots of methods for my students, and in my guides to descriptive writing and writing short stories.

They are the sorts of methods your teachers give you in school. Lots of steps which will make it impossible for you to get a bad mark.

But, that's not what real writers do. And it's also not very easy. It makes writing a bit like a maths problem.

Can I Keep it Simple?

I think I can if I tell you what to do *everywhere* in your writing, whether it is a story or a description. So, there are no steps, apart from the ending.

1. Start each sentence with a different word (as far as possible).
2. Use the big five: *simile, metaphor, personification, alliteration* and *sibilance*. Let's call this *imagery*.
3. Use the best vocabulary you can, but don't use words you aren't familiar with.
4. Have at least one character, so you can always introduce different perspectives, flashbacks, thoughts etc.
5. Use contrast.
6. Use *colon, exclamation mark, question mark, brackets* and *ellipsis*.
7. When you get to the end, refer back in some way to the beginning: this gives you a circular structure.
8. That also works for a story, if you can't think of an ending.

I'm not sure how simple this is. But I do know if you keep practising all 8, you will **never** get a low grade.

When you read the top student answers in this guide, you will see that they all do all of these.

VIPSCCC?

Everyone loves a mnemonic.

Vocabulary, Imagery, Punctuation, Sentence starts, **Character, Contrast, Circular** structure.

Maybe that's not very memorable! But, I think following those steps should b

No Method
Alternatively, just read lots of the good answers and try to write your own versions of them.

Mark Scheme

AO5 Content and Organisation

Compelling, Convincing Communication   **22-24 marks**
1. Extensive and ambitious vocabulary
2. Sustained crafting of linguistic devices
3. Varied and inventive use of structural features
4. Fluently linked paragraphs

Convincing   **19–21 marks**
1-4 above, *but not inventive and compelling*

Consistent, Clear Communication   **16-18 marks**
1. Increasingly sophisticated vocabulary
2. A range of successful linguistic devices
3. Effective use of structural features
4. Paragraphs which make sense in the right order

Clear   **13-15 marks**
1-4 above, *but not always consistent*

Some Successful Communication   **10-12 marks**
1. Trying to use interesting vocabulary
2. Some use of linguistic devices
3. Some use of structural features
4. Some use of paragraphs

Attempts
1-4 are attempted *but are usually not successful*   **7-9 marks**

Simple, Limited Communication   **4-6 marks**
1. Simple vocabulary
2. Simple linguistic devices
3. Simple structure
4. Random paragraphs in the wrong order

Barely Communicates   **1-3 marks**
1. Does not use linguistic devices
2. Does not use paragraphs
3. Doesn't have more than two ideas

AO6 Technical Accuracy and Sentence Variety

Level 4: Imaginative and Accurate   **13-16 marks**
1. Wide range of punctuation is used with a high level of accuracy
2. Uses a full range of appropriate sentence forms for effect
3. Uses Standard English consistently and appropriately
4. No mistakes with grammar
5. Very few mistakes in spelling, including ambitious vocabulary

6. Extensive and ambitious use of vocabulary

Level 3: Usually Imaginative and Usually Accurate   **9-12 marks**
1. A range of punctuation is used, mostly accurate
2. Uses a variety of sentence forms for effect
3. Mostly uses Standard English appropriately
4. Few mistakes in grammar
5. Mostly accurate spelling, including complex and irregular words
6. Increasingly sophisticated use of vocabulary

Level 2: Sometimes Imaginative and Sometimes Accurate   **5-8 marks**
1. Some control of a range of punctuation
2. Attempts a variety of sentence forms
3. Some use of Standard English
4. Some mistakes with tenses or plurals
5. Some accurate spelling of more complex words
6. Varied vocabulary

Level 1: Rarely Imaginative and Rarely Accurate   **1-4 marks**
1. Sentences sometimes miss full stops
2. Some evidence of other punctuation, rarely used correctly
3. Sentences are boring
4. Sometimes uses Standard English
5. Usually makes mistakes with tenses or plurals
6. Accurate basic spelling
7. Simple vocabulary

How to Use the Mark Schemes
1. Read the bold headings.
2. Use your gut instinct to decide which one best describes the writing.
3. Then look at the bullet points under the headings to decide how many marks to give it.
4. If it has every bullet point, look at the level above – if it matches any of those bullet points, decide if it gets partly into the next level.

What have you learned?

1. **Jot down words or phrases to steal.**
2. **Write down ideas, characters, settings, plots you can use in your own writing.**
3. **Write down anything you have learned about the exam, punctuation, spelling.**
4. **Rewrite part of the answer to give it great grades.**

_____

_____

_____

_____

_____

Based on Paper 1 June 2017

The Question

Students had a choice of writing a story about two people from different backgrounds

Or a description of a bus journey, suggested by a picture of people sitting on a bus, at night time. I've changed the description to a journey on a train.

Response 1

A girl called Jemima, who had a rich family, wanted to get into a public school, but unluckily it was full. So Jemima went to her local school. Both her parents regretted this and couldn't educate her at home as they both had jobs. No one paid Jemima much attention at school as she got bullied for her poshness. A large girl called Jay approached her. She lived down the hill in a poor part where Jemima lived up the hill. They liked each other and started to play. While Jemima came home and told her parents about this friend, they weren't very happy about Jay's hair colour and they said it's best not to see her. So when Jay asked to play with Jemima, Jemima told her to go away. Jemima didn't want to make Jay feel alone but she wanted to obey her parents if not to be punished.

Then their teacher put Jemima and Jay together in a pair for a reading task. Jemima was into Harry Potter while Jay was really into Lord of the Rings.

180 words

AO5 6

Original AO6 6

My Commentary

AO5

1. The examiner decided this is simple and limited and doesn't attempt to do anything interesting.

2. Although the second paragraph is correct, there are several changes of time where there should have been other paragraphs.

3. However, the student does try to use the right vocabulary and to write some varied sentences. This is why the AO6 mark was higher (even before I corrected the punctuation so you can see the sentence structures).

Simple, Limited Communication   **4-6 marks**
- Simple vocabulary
- Simple linguistic devices
- Simple structure
- Random paragraphs in the wrong order – this is the greatest strength in AO5 – the order does make sense, but it is not enough given how limited the rest is.

AO6

Level 2: Sometimes Imaginative and Sometimes Accurate   5-8 marks

- Attempts a variety of sentence forms – notice that they have done this by trying to start sentences with different words.
- Some use of Standard English
- Some mistakes with tenses or plurals
- Varied vocabulary – the student hasn't thought hard about their choice of vocabulary yet

What have you learned?

1. **Jot down words or phrases to steal.**
2. **Write down ideas, characters, settings, plots you can use in your own writing.**
3. **Write down anything you have learned about the exam, punctuation, spelling.**
4. **Rewrite part of the answer to give it great grades.**

_____

_____

_____

_____

_____

_____

_____

_____

_____

_____

_____

_____

_____

_____

_____

_____

_____

_____

_____

_____

_____

_____

_____

Response 2

Poor people and rich people have different lives.

A woman called Julia Jones was a successful dentist who lived in the countryside. Her home was luxurious and huge which was in the middle of delightful views. In the scenery there were wide open fields with beautifully coloured crops growing everywhere.

Julia was lucky as she could have every advantage at her fingertips as her parents were successful in their careers. Her parents bought her an expensive thoroughbred horse which was as quick as a plane. The horse was as white as snow and the large muscles rippled with lines as it ran along the densely growing fields.

Julia's mansion was as big as the houses of parliament and its rooms had more colours than a rainbow.

Julia attended a public school which gave her a beneficial education.

There was another girl called Elizabeth. Elizabeth was a royal who had many homes and her family was in Paris. Her parents died one day when Elizabeth was 13 and she was left without any support. She became homeless and began to beg. She was like a tiny ragdoll who had no food or money and no change of clothes and no shoes in her possession.

She had green eyes and dark hair and was very delicate like the wings of a swan. She was especially sickly and many times had to scavenge for food in household bins.

For years Elizabeth lived on the streets of Paris, becoming a pick pocket, stealing from the very wealthy and eating scraps.

256 words

AO5 9

Original AO6 8

My Commentary

AO5:

1. The student is trying to use interesting vocabulary and interesting sentences. This is just more than sometimes, so it just sneaks into the next mark band.

2. They have tried to introduce an interesting contrast between Julia and Elizabeth.

3. The similes are boring, but the student is trying to use them to help us picture what they are describing.

This is what is missing:

Some Successful Communication	**10-12 marks**
<ul><li>Trying to use interesting vocabulary</li><li>Some use of linguistic devices</li><li>Some use of structural features</li><li>Some use of paragraphs</li></ul>	

Attempts This is where the answer is:
1-4 are attempted but are usually not successful   **7-9 marks**

Simple, Limited Communication   **4-6 marks**
1. Simple vocabulary
2. Simple linguistic devices
3. Simple structure
4. Random paragraphs in the wrong order

AO6:

1. The errors in the original kept the score down.

2. Even now, we can see that there is no variety in the punctuation.

3. Every sentence starts in a predictable way.

4. The vocabulary choices are the strongest feature, followed by having lots of accurate paragraphs.

This is what is missing:
- Uses a variety of sentence forms for effect
- Mostly uses Standard English appropriately
- Few mistakes in grammar
- Increasingly sophisticated use of vocabulary

5-8 marks – This is where the answer is:
- Attempts a variety of sentence forms
- Some use of Standard English
- Some mistakes with tenses or plurals
- Varied vocabulary

What have you learned?

1. **Jot down words or phrases to steal.**
2. **Write down ideas, characters, settings, plots you can use in your own writing.**
3. **Write down anything you have learned about the exam, punctuation, spelling.**
4. **Rewrite part of the answer to give it great grades.**

_____

_____

_____

_____

_____

_____

I waited for the train. Never on time! I got on the train and sat, near the window of course, at the best seat I find. The trip was going to be long. The train was pretty full. It was quiet. I wanted to listen to music with my headphones. As the songs play, I'm looking at the fields passing by so quick. All I notice is a blur of countryside. I loved watching through the window. I saw trees swaying slowly in the breeze, birds in the sky, and leaves dancing around in unison. Then a woman pushed passed my table and sat in front of me. A scent of perfume filled the carriage and made me want to sneeze. I glance at the carriage. It was crowded. Laptops all over the tables, ruck sacks on the seating, passengers eating, some standing in the aisle. I stop listening to music to concentrate on what I can see. As I take my headphones off, the noise of a baby's cries and wails surrounding the passengers, I moved closer to the window, resting my gaze on the pleasant green fields. The train pulled in. Passengers got on. One teenager on a call sat in front of me and two small boys sit down near the front. The train starts with a huge pull. While this happens, someone's shoulder bashes into a passenger and many of them scatter down the aisle. The passengers were fumbling and grabbing to get back on their feet. Some passengers watched with amusement. No one helped.

Station by station the crowded old train was emptying, getting quieter and quieter. People working, sleeping and texting. A few passengers talking, a few drinking and finishing cold coffees before leaving their seats. This was the best time to be on the train. The mood was calm. It was now a short trip.

312 words

AO5 11

Original AO6 7

My Commentary

AO5:

1. Trying to use interesting vocabulary

2. Some use of linguistic devices

3. Some use of structural features

4. Some use of paragraphs – this is the feature that has cost the student most marks. Two doesn't really qualify as 'some', so they haven't even got into this band for paragraphing. This is what stops them having 12 marks.

Some Successful Communication	10-12 marks

1. Trying to use interesting vocabulary
2. Some use of linguistic devices
3. Some use of structural features
4. Some use of paragraphs

AO6

1. The most obvious thing holding the writer back is 'Some mistakes with tenses or plurals'. Switching between past and present tenses is incredibly common, and so easy to fix.

2. Next time you practise your writing, underline every verb. Then change the ones which are in the wrong tense. You could start by doing that with this writing. After 4-6 goes at this, you should be cured forever.

Level 2: Sometimes Imaginative and Sometimes Accurate   **5-8 marks**
- Attempts a variety of sentence forms
- Some use of Standard English
- Some mistakes with tenses or plurals
- Varied vocabulary

What have you learned?

1. Jot down words or phrases to steal.
2. Write down ideas, characters, settings, plots you can use in your own writing.
3. Write down anything you have learned about the exam, punctuation, spelling.
4. Rewrite part of the answer to give it great grades.

_____

_____

_____

_____

_____

Response 4

I sat in the train returning home, trapped by passengers from every part of the city. The train was mainly full of men with their over filled rucksacks and their newspapers. The carriage started to get crowded, which made me angry as I am quite large. I usually end up sitting next to a shy, embarrassed teenager. Today, no one sat next to me.

Then a fat woman came down the aisle.

"Damn it," I thought, as I imagined her route. She would sit with me. She began to wobble slowly toward my seat, so I glared at the view of the peaceful countryside and folded my arms.

It was Saturday, so the train was crammed with passengers getting drunk. The carriage was filled with laughter and chatter.

Just then the train passed something strange. A woman wearing black on a ladder.

She suddenly climbed into a window. Was that her house? I had to get off the train, but was trapped by the wobbling woman. I pushed my way to the exit, but her great lump was like a pudding to push by.

I gradually gave in and stayed in my seat. I had to do something. I tried to be more confident.

"I'd like to get off the train please," I said loudly.

Her knees cracked and creaked as she stood up. I got to the door while we were still at the station. Then the train pulled away.

I found the exit and began to run to the house with the ladder. It was at least half a mile so I paced my speed.

A few minutes later, I arrived at the house. I could see a light moving in the house, searching for something. Why was I the only one who noticed? I wondered.

Then the woman came down the ladder carrying a large case. I shuffled into the garden hoping not to be seen.

319 words

AO5 13

Original AO6 9

My Commentary

AO5

The writing does all of the following, which is worth 12 marks.

1. Trying to use interesting vocabulary

2. Some use of linguistic devices

3. Some use of structural features

4. Some use of paragraphs

Which one of these does the student do best? It is the paragraphing, which lifts it one mark into the next band. This is what the student needs to do next.

1. Increasingly sophisticated vocabulary: the easiest way to do this is simply to start each sentence with a different word.

2. A range of successful linguistic devices: this means the **big five: *simile, metaphor, personification, alliteration and sibilance*.**

3. Effective use of structural features: the weakness here is that the ending is rushed, so there is no point to it. The other issue is that it happens at random. It would have been far easier to introduce someone suspicious on the train, who the narrator follows to the platform – with a twist – perhaps the narrator switches bags with them, and turns out to be a criminal. This can be difficult to write though.

   So the easiest way to introduce structural features is to introduce the **character's thoughts and memories**. The second easiest is to use **contrast**.

AO6

The original writing did all of these:
1. Some control of a range of punctuation

2. Attempts a variety of sentence forms

3. Some use of Standard English

4. Some mistakes with tenses or plurals

5. Some accurate spelling of more complex words

6. Varied vocabulary

They moved into the next band because there were no mistakes with tenses and plurals.

The easiest way to move up the mark scheme would be to focus on:

1. A range of punctuation is used, mostly accurate.
   The best way to do this is to be quite mechanical about it – make sure to use **one** of these in every bit of writing: ***colon, question mark, ellipsis, exclamation mark***. It is more difficult, but essential, to learn to use commas properly.

2. Uses a variety of sentence forms for effect.
   Well, you know this by now: start as many sentences as you can with a different word. Notice that using the 4 pieces of punctuation in point 1 will also automatically vary your sentence forms! Win, win.

Jude hunched over at the back of the carriage. His hands were frozen fists and he sat rigidly as an ice sculpture. He slowly scanned the carriage like a small child waiting for bullies to leave the playground. The seats in front were empty except for two men at the front. The one by the window was yelling furiously at the mobile – maybe a wife or child. In front of him a teenager was engrossed in the neon advertising scrolling by outside. The aging slow train ground to a halt at a station. The males left the train swiftly and a young woman glided on gracefully. An alarm bell sounded in Jude's mind. He remember her. She was the girl who had dumped him at school. Sweat as wet as Vaseline coated his flesh. Hair stood up on his cold pasty skin. As silently as possible, he pressed himself into his old threadbare seat and held his breath. He observed her through the small gap in the seating hiding him. Her black eyeliner was alarming. She wore an angry expression and looked alert.

Just fifteen minutes to go. Then he would be free. He slowly turned his gaze to the view outside. The countryside had disappeared and the train crawled closer to his station.

Just ten minutes to go. The train slid towards home. He loved the anonymity of the town coming to his rescue at such an embarrassing moment.

Just five minutes to go. He began to prepare his exit. He silently moved his backpack onto his lap and quietly zipped up his jacket.

As the train slowed to a halt, he stood. He stumbled. And her eyes looked into his own.

283 words

AO5 15

Original AO6 12

My Commentary

AO5

The answer does all of the following, *but not consistently*:

1. Increasingly sophisticated vocabulary – you can pick out the words you notice and try to use them yourself in a short piece of writing. However, notice how many sentences begin with the same words. This stops it being consistently sophisticated in using vocabulary.

2. A range of successful linguistic devices – you should be able to spot some simile and alliteration. There are probably too many adverbs, which is nearly always a sign of writing which is not consistent – it feels as though it is trying too hard to show off.

3. Effective use of structural features – check out the final paragraphs. The simple idea of a count down works, doesn't it? Notice how the sentences get shorter at the end to increase the tension of the moment when their eyes meet.

4. Paragraphs which make sense in the right order – notice that for more than half of the answer the student is just writing without thinking about paragraphs – they are thinking of describing. This is normal under exam pressure, but shows the importance of checking for paragraphing in the exam.

I suspect the student didn't know at the start of their writing that the intimidating woman was going to get on the train. Once the student introduced this character, they had an ending in mind. This is also typical in an exam. If you can plan your ending from the start, your writing will improve.

If you start without knowing the end, your beginning is likely to be worse than the second half of your writing. Understand this, and keep some time to go back to the first half to correct paragraphs and duff description.

Or, simply plan to have two characters in every story, which will make it 100% likely that you will be able to contrast them. This contrast will automatically introduce tension and help you think up an ending as you are writing.

AO6

The main areas to focus on for moving up to the next band are:

1. Wide range of punctuation is used with a high level of accuracy
2. Uses a full range of appropriate sentence forms for effect

The easiest way to practise for punctuation is just to force yourself to use those I listed earlier – **colon, question mark, exclamation mark** and **ellipsis**. You can add brackets or dashes to this list. Don't use semi-colons unless you really know what you are doing – students mostly get these completely wrong.

Notice that just starting each sentence with a different word will force your writing to have a large range of sentence forms.

What have you learned?

1. **Jot down words or phrases to steal.**
2. **Write down ideas, characters, settings, plots you can use in your own writing.**
3. **Write down anything you have learned about the exam, punctuation, spelling.**
4. **Rewrite part of the answer to give it great grades.**

_____

_____

_____

_____

_____

_____

_____

_____

_____

_____

Life never changes.

As the dry, **coughing splutter** of the diesel engine dragged the wheels below the commuters of the London train, the vast suburbs slid by them (the same as every other day).

Though **the moon had conquered the sky** not long ago, **London elbowed into the train** with a bright presence.

Neon.

A source of light and joy – but not tonight. Not here. Not for this train. As the train trundled onwards, the prying gaze of streetlights and illuminated high-rises assaulted the exhausted observer. Pathetic wails for assistance came from the emergency vehicles, and the *honking of horns* intruded from the one busted *window which wouldn't* close.

Would life always be like this?

Beyond the train **breathed an uncaring, unstoppable monster**: London. **It was an enemy**. Nothing less. **Trucks screeched angrily on the roads**, and crowded, **drone-filled tenements jostled the streets like bee-hives**. Occasional fools (the young) were happy. It was close to miserable. They were mistaken – they just had to gaze upwards.

Within the oblong, steel train, was a microcosm of London life. Sitting awkwardly on the vilely patterned seating were passengers … But they were barely human, weren't they?

They were lifeless.

Dead.

Many of these strange creatures had closed their eyes, while many more fought hopelessly to stay alert. Perhaps sleep was better.

Nevertheless, sleep didn't prevent the harsh, riotous sounds **of the monster outside** from meeting their ears, uninvited. What allowed this ordinary experience of their miserable living to be so depressing?

Beyond the *dark, dilapidated* slums, **the monster had built** a new construction: **a cloud catcher. This skyscraper created its own reputation, intrusively attracting clouds** against a once cloudless sky, obliterating light with its ungodly form. Circling the ground floor of this construction were numberless screens, *pulsating unwelcome products* onto the empty gazes of the passers-by.

Spend now! It will fulfil you! Don't you need this immediately?

How true.

Londoners wanted happiness.

Yet the giant dark shade enveloping the train from the skyscraper did not bring happiness. Condensation dripped gradually across the windows of the carriage like smeared Vaseline. The train's front had a *lone light* which was smashed. Silently, the cracked light dimmed, circled by the dazzling, neon lights, as though it was **as abandoned as the passengers** in the train.

On the horizon, a strange form could be made out. It was a mound. Green, rising from the fields that welcomed the travellers who ended their almost eternal journey.

It was waiting.

Satisfied desire.

It had always been here.

AO5 20

Original AO6 15

My Commentary

AO5

Ok, let's start with the positives.

1. The writing is all based around contrast.

2. The student is constantly thinking about using interesting vocabulary.

3. They keep varying the length of sentences.

4. It uses a range of sounds.

5. It uses metaphors and similes.

Convincing	**19–21 marks**

1-4 above, *but not inventive and compelling*

Consistent, Clear Communication	**16-18 marks**

1. Increasingly sophisticated vocabulary
2. A range of successful linguistic devices
3. Effective use of structural features
4. Paragraphs which make sense in the right order

AO6

Level 4: Imaginative and Accurate
13-16 marks

1. Wide range of punctuation is used with a high level of accuracy
2. Uses a full range of appropriate sentence forms for effect
3. Uses Standard English consistently and appropriately
4. No mistakes with grammar
5. Very few mistakes in spelling, including ambitious vocabulary
6. Extensive and ambitious use of vocabulary

These marks are pretty good! But, it is horrible writing.

This is why the AO5 mark is not yet inventive and compelling: it is completely over the top, crammed with descriptions you would never read in a novel. It actually upsets me deeply that teachers teach description this way. But it is not all their fault – they teach this way because it can lead to good exam grades. So I blame the exam boards.

But I beg you not to do it. The experience will either make you dislike writing, or develop terrible habits which will hold you back. Read on to see how better student writers do it.

What have you learned?

1. Jot down words or phrases to steal.
2. Write down ideas, characters, settings, plots you can use in your own writing.
3. Write down anything you have learned about the exam, punctuation, spelling.
4. Rewrite part of the answer to give it great grades.

_____
_____
_____
_____
_____
_____
_____
_____
_____
_____
_____
_____
_____
_____
_____
_____
_____
_____
_____
_____
_____
_____
_____
_____

Here's the same description, rewritten as it might appear in a novel.

Evie longed for a better life.

The commuter train left London slowly, **dragging itself through the city, crawling towards the suburbs**. She had worked late, again. She looked out of the windows dazzled with headlights and neon, caught in the rain. **The wailing of an ambulance pleaded to be let through** the gridlock outside.

Would life always be like this, she *wondered.*

She tried to see the scene differently, but London **sprang up all around the tracks** in gaudy excess. **The skyline jostled**, full of *sky scrapers scarcely* a decade old, and **a forest of cranes threatened** many more.

She turned to the passengers, to see if they were coping any better than she was. But their impassive faces looked grey; the blue light of their phones illuminated them **like ghosts**. She stopped herself, aware that she was over dramatising the journey.

But, as she *scanned the carriage, she counted* those with their eyes shut, their mouths going slack. Not dead, but sleeping. But this wasn't living, was it? It was wishing the time away, longing for somewhere else.

She looked out again, into the London night, and the still lit office blocks passed by. **Billboards flashed their desperate messages**. Your life is dreary, they said, but all this can change with a whitened *smile, a new dress, a slow cruise*, Bitcoin…

Annoyed at her inability to think positively, Evie instead looked at her *reflection in the rain* steaked windows. Lights **smeared across the pane like Vaseline**. She wondered if anyone had ever described the rain on a *window in these words* before. It seemed, at last, like a fresh idea.

Outside, **the suburbs were creeping into view**. Evie pictured a character, suddenly waking up on a train, with no memory of who they were or where they had been. She could see the woman clearly, going home to the suburbs, to a husband and toddler she wouldn't recognise.

Yes, she had the first line of her novel. She would begin writing it tomorrow, on the slow return journey back to London.

Evie got off the train and smiled for the first time that day.

Tomorrow would be utterly different.

My Commentary

1. As you can see, it has exactly the same scene and much of the same language and imagery.

2. Introducing a character makes the description meaningful, and also helps it feel as though it will fit in a novel.

3. Like the original (and like all good writing), it relies on contrast. But the contrast helps us understand the character as well as picture the scene.

4. Although it is shorter, it will score full marks.

5. (My only compromise is making sure that the examiner can't deduct marks for not using enough punctuation. The semi-colon doesn't feel as natural as using 'and' instead, but I've had to include it for that reason. The ellipsis does work, as it suggests that Evie could keep listing the dozens of products being advertised).

6. It uses 8 similes or metaphors, which fit the story. The previous version uses 14, many of which don't fit. Go back and see how I have changed them.

What have you learned?

1. **Jot down words or phrases to steal.**
2. **Write down ideas, characters, settings, plots you can use in your own writing.**
3. **Write down anything you have learned about the exam, punctuation, spelling.**
4. **Rewrite part of the answer to give it great grades.**

_____

_____

_____

_____

_____

_____

_____

_____

_____

_____

_____

_____

_____

_____

_____

_____

_____

_____

_____

_____

_____

Based on Paper 1 June 2020

The Question

Students had the choice to write a story about an event which couldn't be explained.

Or they could write a description about a mysterious place. They were presented with a picture of metal gates inside a stone arch, with mist and trees in the background.

Response 2

On this misty and foggy morning one day, my sisters and me was walking a little way into the woods. We was pretty nervous, as it was foggy and all we could see was mist, so we began to play tig and I got chosen to be it.

But I was nervous because I thought I might get lost and I didn't want to play. So I started the count. And as soon as I got to 10 I opened my eyes. I decided to go straight ahead as I couldn't tell which way to turn.

I've been searching for ages and I didn't find them. As I searched I saw a barn door which opened, so I said to myself, "well, if the door is open they must have gone inside."

So I went in and it was empty. And I heard things. Something yelling. So began to walk out of there. As I got to the barn door it shut. It was so fast I couldn't get out. So I'm trapped and couldn't work out what next.

So I yelled, "help me!" hoping that my friends would save me.

Half an hour in there. They finally got me out and I was like, "don't ever let me come back."

A05 7

Original AO6 6

My Commentary

AO5

The key question is how far this communication is successful and how far it is limited. Well, the examiner has placed it one mark into successful. This is because there is a beginning, middle and end.

Everything else is limited, because:

1. The tenses keep changing.
2. Most sentences begin with the same word.

Some Successful Communication
1. Trying to use interesting vocabulary
2. Some use of linguistic devices

3. Some use of structural features
4. Some use of paragraphs

1-4 are attempted *but are usually not successful* **7-9 marks**

AO6

1. The original was one long paragraph

2. There were hardly any full stops, with many replaced by commas

Level 2: Sometimes Imaginative and Sometimes Accurate   5-8 marks
1. Some control of a range of punctuation – notice the speech marks and exclamation mark, which were used by the student.
2. Attempts a variety of sentence forms – you can see this in the sentences with clauses, even though they didn't use commas properly in the original.
3. Some use of Standard English
4. Some mistakes with tenses or plurals
5. Some accurate spelling of more complex words
6. Varied vocabulary – well, perhaps misty and foggy count?

What have you learned?

1. Jot down words or phrases to steal.
2. Write down ideas, characters, settings, plots you can use in your own writing.
3. Write down anything you have learned about the exam, punctuation, spelling.
4. Rewrite part of the answer to give it great grades.

_____

_____

_____

_____

_____

_____

_____

_____

_____

_____

_____

_____

_____

_____

_____

_____

_____

_____

Response 3

It was a black, freezing night about 10 o'clock. I chose to try a walk as home was boring. I went out, leaving my hat in the house, because it was a really freezing evening.

I begin strolling to the shops and saw a track what goes into the coal dark forest. I decided I must walk in there, so I went in cautiously inside the black forest with my torch from my mobile.

So I went about half an hour in the forest to look for another track to walk along. And I said, I'll find out what's there and 400 meters down the path it began to be really rainy and the wind was blowing.

I turned around. And I was surprised. There was a large brick arch what I hadn't even see. There was a crow on the arch what made me cautious going under.

I turned and went to leave and the door opened before I even reached it. So I glanced through the archway to see a path of bare trees and long waving branches. And the wind pounding through the branches created a whining kind of howl. What howled everywhere. I was intrigued to go wander but was really anxious.

But all of a sudden a branch crashed in front of me blocking the track, so I had to go on another path. The longer I strolled the more noises I heard ahead of me. Right now I'm astonished and concerned for whatever is ahead. The noises I heard was screaming just howling through the woods. I didn't have any food and wanted to eat.

I needed to turn back but could not as the track was under the fallen tree. Getting closer, I imagined I saw someone, a small girl. She was about 11 years old in fact. Long blonde plaits, clothed in a ragged second hand dress.

I yelled in astonishment. At once she began running. At the same time I had no choices. Perhaps she knows another path. So I ran after her.

342 words

A05 10

Original AO6 7

My Commentary

AO5

1. This has the same weaknesses as the previous answer. But there are more sentences which start with different words. There are just as many which don't, but because this is longer, there are more examples of success.

2. The same is true of mistakes with tenses – there are quite a few, but because there are more sentences, there are more examples of correct use of tenses.

3. Playing around with vocabulary means that some of the sentences are interesting to read.

4. The student has introduced sounds quite well, because the sounds help us picture the scene. None of the description feels as though it is only there to prove that the student is describing.

Some Successful Communication   **10-12 marks**
1. Trying to use interesting vocabulary – you will spot quite a bit in the second paragraph
2. Some use of linguistic devices – in particular the sounds.
3. Some use of structural features – look at the repetition. It has a clear beginning, but not a clear ending.
4. Some use of paragraphs

AO6

1. The original had 4 paragraphs, so the student is thinking about how to help the reader spot changes of time.

2. The structure is chronological which helps make the story clearer, despite the changes in tenses.

3. Notice that vocabulary gets marks in both AO6 and AO5. This student is really trying to use interesting vocabulary and sometimes this is successful.

Level 2: Sometimes Imaginative and Sometimes Accurate   5-8 marks

1. Some control of a range of punctuation
2. Attempts a variety of sentence forms
3. Some use of Standard English
4. Some mistakes with tenses or plurals
5. Some accurate spelling of more complex words
6. Varied vocabulary

What have you learned?

1. Jot down words or phrases to steal.
2. Write down ideas, characters, settings, plots you can use in your own writing.
3. Write down anything you have learned about the exam, punctuation, spelling.
4. Rewrite part of the answer to give it great grades.

_____

_____

_____

_____

_____

_____

_____

_____

Response 4

Black, freezing, soaking darkness. Simply walking the area I've come to live in. Exploring, looking for something to walk around.

Strolling about for some time by now, I am bored and have found nobody to see. As I'm strolling I can make out a barrier with keep out. So I walk to it. As I come closer to this "forbid" area, you go in through a semi-circle of stones.

It seemed when I enter the semi-circle of stones, I enter an alternative universe or whatever. Peering into the area I can only see lots of weeds, which is up to your waist like. Weeds everywhere. Can't see inside the place. And it is totally dark, just no light.

Walking into the strange zone, I was nervous. Even strolling into these weeds and walking among the flowers I couldn't see which paths to follow.

I cannot choose.

I keep on the same path and shadows suddenly come quickly, like animals are circling around me and I am caught in a trap. So I ask myself, is this smart? And I stop. Should I leave this place?

The rumbling of six branches and the cracking of the flowers. I am sure an animal is coming. I look to one side and see a dog that looks like its creeping through the weeds. Hair all standing up, teeth showing, eyes watching and paws all padding towards me.

I tell him to stop there. Why is it here?

It growls at me and just keeps coming.

252 words

AO5 12

Original AO6 8

My Commentary

AO5

1. You might feel the same way I do about this. I thought the previous answer was a better read. It made more sense. I could picture the scene more clearly.

2. So, what is better in this piece? What has influenced the examiner?

- It is the number of sentences which start with a different word.
- And the number of short sentences to build a sense of drama towards the end.

Some Successful Communication   **10-12 marks**
1. Trying to use interesting vocabulary – look at the paragraph which starts 'The rumbling...'
2. Some use of linguistic devices – there is an attempt at one simile – spot the 'like'.
3. Some use of structural features – this is really just starting sentences in lots of different ways. Making one a question also helps. Varying the length of sentences also helps.
4. Some use of paragraphs

AO6

1. The student wrote 4 paragraphs.

2. They are trying to vary their vocabulary, with a similar success rate to the previous answer.

Level 2: Sometimes Imaginative and Sometimes Accurate   5-8 marks
1. Some control of a range of punctuation
2. Attempts a variety of sentence forms – see point 3 in AO5 above.
3. Some use of Standard English
4. Some mistakes with tenses or plurals
5. Some accurate spelling of more complex words
6. Varied vocabulary – again, you can see how this pays off in both AO5 and AO6, so it gets rewarded twice! See point 1 in AO5.

What have you learned?

1. **Jot down words or phrases to steal.**
2. **Write down ideas, characters, settings, plots you can use in your own writing.**
3. **Write down anything you have learned about the exam, punctuation, spelling.**
4. **Rewrite part of the answer to give it great grades.**

_____

_____

_____

_____

_____

_____

_____

_____

_____

_____

_____

_____

_____

_____

_____

_____

_____

_____

_____

_____

Response 5

Waiting at the turnstiles of the zoo, I'm certain I shouldn't enter. The zoo had been empty for a decade, abandoned with no one keepers left in it.

The grass is overgrown with weeds giving it a sense of spookiness. Everybody knows that the zoo houses some remaining animals, some dangerous and vicious. I waited, deciding whether to enter to find my puppy, or waiting for it to choose to return home.

Weighing up these decisions and ruminating, I could perceive movement in one of the enclosures. The lighting inside was poor. So you wouldn't be able to make out what was inside. Yet the movements were sudden as a cobra. Yet the decaying tree which appeared as a malformed fist obstructed my view of what hid within.

All of a sudden, the cobra like movements in the enclosure sped towards me and I was sure it would attack me like a cheetah would leap on its victim. While I remained standing, trying not identify it, I knew it would slaughter me.

Expecting to be torn to shreds, praying for help, a different shape jumped into view and pounced on the predator as it rushed at me.

Finally I understood. A wolf was stalking me but a lion devoured the wolf and unintentionally saved me.

196 words

A05 14

AO6 9

My Commentary

Consistent, Clear Communication   **16-18 marks**
1. Increasingly sophisticated vocabulary – you can see that the students has thought carefully about at least two words in every line. Look at the last line – stalking, devoured, unintentionally.
2. A range of successful linguistic devices – the cobra is used for two similes. The malformed fist is a metaphor stolen from Source A in the reading questions! Yes, that is allowed – see my notes on plagiarism. Probably not enough for a range.
3. Effective use of structural features – there is a clear beginning, middle and end, but no other interesting aspects of structure.
4. Paragraphs which make sense in the right order

Clear   **13-15 marks**
1-4 above, but not always consistent

AO6

Level 3: Usually Imaginative and Usually Accurate   **9-12 marks**
- A range of punctuation is used, mostly accurate
- Uses a variety of sentence forms for effect – which you remember is simply starting sentences with a different word. And then mixing up short and long sentences. You can see that the long ones give great detail about the threat, but also delay that threat happening.

So, by mistake, the student has reduced the tension. Sometimes, faster pace, shorter sentences do that better.

- Mostly uses Standard English appropriately
- Few mistakes in grammar
- Mostly accurate spelling, including complex and irregular words
- Increasingly sophisticated use of vocabulary

What have you learned?

1. **Jot down words or phrases to steal.**
2. **Write down ideas, characters, settings, plots you can use in your own writing.**
3. **Write down anything you have learned about the exam, punctuation, spelling.**
4. **Rewrite part of the answer to give it great grades.**

_____

_____

_____

_____

_____

_____

_____

_____

_____

_____

_____

_____

_____

_____

_____

_____

_____

_____

_____

_____

_____

_____

_____

Response 6

Just two years ago, a fox's sudden howl was eerie and creates a strange feeling on an outing with my family. As I collect my bags from the laid back and casual taxi driver, I receive a goodbye from the cab, skidding like a skater slipping on ice in their first lesson.

Darkness has fallen.

Carefully but hopeful I start to pick a route down the rough and muddy track to be astonished by an archway like the entrance to Rome! Majestic and towering, rounded and ancient.

The arch didn't invite me any more. I won't accept that this ancient, delightful building has become desolate over time. I can't see beyond its doors. Only the moon guides me. By which I imagine disaster could truly be beyond those doors.

A sharp and sudden snap slowly echoes to my ears. As the sounds disappear, a new twisting track is my new destination. The further and further I go, I am more and more anxious and scared.

An unexpected fall helps me truly notice where I am. I get up surrounded by darkness, as my pupils widen to cope with the light. How is this happening?

Branches reach out to me like hands clutching at my clothes. Panic fills my mind as hand after hand reaches out for me. Cautiously, I start off once more in the cosy quiet.

I look further ahead to the frightening, bendy imposing trees. Once more I'm attacked by a sense of panic as I remember being mugged in a dark, deserted park.

They aren't trees as I start to shake and sweat profusely. A steel fence stood between me and escape. The archway is my goal I think. I battle through the trees still remembering my scream and fear.

My bag is my shield and my pen is my sword. I run to attack and attack and attack ... then what? I am at the archway, welcomed by a door with a weird carving on each.

'1894 – 1918 a life well lived,' I read in large letters.

I start to hear sobs and the voice of a man.

"Aha," I hear myself saying...

"Rest in peace James Watson, an optimist."

364 words

A05 17

Original AO6 11

My commentary

AO5

1. The student starts sentences with different words much more frequently.

32

2. As well as focusing on sound vocabulary, the student has started to add alliteration.

3. They are trying to use a range of similes and metaphors, which try to match the topic of the description.

4. The student had been taught to introduce a memory or a flashback, which will help describe the present scene.

5. They've started to use adjectives in pairs to give a more interesting picture of each thing.

6. The students is trying to vary the grammar and word order of sentences, so that they are not predictable.

7. The student has tried to craft an ending, even though it doesn't fully make sense.

8. The description might be confusing in places, but it is much more detailed.

Consistent, Clear Communication   **16-18 marks**
1. Increasingly sophisticated vocabulary – see points 1 and 6 above
2. A range of successful linguistic devices – see points 3 and 5 above
3. Effective use of structural features – see points 1, 4 and 7 above
4. Paragraphs which make sense in the right order

AO6

1. The original had 6 paragraphs to help show the reader changes of topic, time and talk.

2. The vocabulary is often chosen to sound sophisticated, although there are some mistakes where words are used in a weird, contradictory way.

3. The student has been trained to use an ellipsis, a question mark and an exclamation mark, whatever the question. Because they are used correctly, they are a range of punctuation.

4. There are fewer errors with tenses, because there are many more sentences.

Level 3: Usually Imaginative and Usually Accurate   **9-12 marks**
1. A range of punctuation is used, mostly accurate
2. Uses a variety of sentence forms for effect
3. Mostly uses Standard English appropriately
4. Few mistakes in grammar
5. Mostly accurate spelling, including complex and irregular words
6. Increasingly sophisticated use of vocabulary

Parliament was chaotic. Government was almost suspended, and a lockdown was being considered.

Whitehall had vanished.

Mercifully, the timetabled motion had been about increased welfare for the disabled. Consequently parliament was virtually empty when the buildings disappeared.

The investigation was shambolic. The search was the equivalent of looking for Downing Street under a sofa – so there was no clear record of the identity of who had vanished.

What of the MPs who remain? Are they still sitting members of parliament if parliament has no seats? One MP suggested meeting on the green, but the presence of the news media put a stop to that. Rumours of a biased press.

Unsurprisingly, the papers were full of expert opinion about the disappearance. It seemed implausible that the whole of Whitehall had put on a zero gravity suit and jumped on a rocket to Mars. Many of the fatter MPs wouldn't have found a suit to fit them. Some other explanation had to be on offer.

Citizens clicked their way across the web, in search of the back benches which had suddenly disapparated. How would the political parties engage in meaningful debate if they had to shout at each other from either side of Westminster bridge? Fortunately, not a single female MP had vanished, so many wondered if the country would be better off.

This morning, a new development occurred; dramatic news (considering what little had been known, a single footprint would have been a headline). Everyone of the missing was discovered in an Amazon fulfilment centre, in boxes marked "CHINA".

That's the breaking news. Architects have already begun to prepare new plans. And -

Hold on.

I've checked the view once more.

Parliament is back.

I'm running to it now. Some sign, some clue as to the disappearance has to be there. Something is stuck to the door. Let me see.

A card? How odd. Who had time to print a message?

Wait, what?

"Mars can do without you…

Love, Elon!"

387 words

A05 20

Original AO6 14

My Commentary

AO5

Writing should be fun. Humour is a great way to access top grades, so long as it is appropriate.

Although this student understands a lot about politics, the plot would work just as well if they had decided to get rid of any public building – Buckingham Palace, the stadium of your favourite football team (or the team you most dislike!) even AQA headquarters...

You can see that they have built the piece around the main joke, that the MPs wouldn't even be welcome on Mars, and a second joke that women MPs are clearly better than male MPs, while the third joke is that Elon Musk is a scientific genius who may not turn out to be a criminal mastermind. (I've made video on the secret sauce of Question 5, and Elon Musk features heavily). You will spot other bits of wordplay too.

The writing is still a little clumsy in the way it suddenly lurches into live action reporting – it would be better all told in the past tense. Perhaps it would be even more dramatic in the present tense, in which case the student could have written it by a live reporter, at the scene on College Green, reporting on the search so far.

You can see that the student is always looking for the right vocabulary. Sentences start with different words. They vary the sentence lengths to build suspense, or emphasise their humour.

Notice that alliteration is really the only descriptive technique, yet it still scores very highly. That said, when you read the next piece, you'll see that the examiner really, really wants you to use some simile or metaphor, to prove that you can write descriptively. This student could do this in a useful way, to emphasise the humour.

For example: "How would the political parties engage in meaningful debate if they had to shout at each other from either side of Westminster bridge *like drunk uncles at a wedding in Magaluf.*"

Compelling, Convincing Communication   **22-24 marks**
1. Extensive and ambitious vocabulary
2. Sustained crafting of linguistic devices
3. Varied and inventive use of structural features
4. Fluently linked paragraphs

Convincing   **19–21 marks**
1-4 above, *but not inventive and compelling*

We can't say it isn't inventive. But the examiner has decided it can't be compelling because of the clumsy narrative voice. This is also means that the structural features are inventive, but not successful enough – an invention which doesn't quite work!

And then there's point 2 – those pesky examiners really want a range of the **big five** devices. You remember what they are, right?

AO6

There is a deliberate range of punctuation – the dashes, ellipsis and exclamation marks are used correctly. They also fit the meaning, they aren't just introduced as part of a checklist. Although, these also appear right at the end, so it may be that the student also did it because they felt they had to get them in regardless. Though real writers wouldn't do this, it is a good technique for the examiner. Sad, but true.

The semi-colon is nearly always used incorrectly by students – it joins two related sentences together. But if the second sentence is an explanation, use the colon. So, they should have written "a new development occurred: dramatic news".

You know by now that vocabulary counts twice. This is another advantage of having some expert knowledge about a subject – even a student who knows nothing about politics, but everything about Manchester United would be able to pepper their writing with advanced vocabulary relevant to football – *director, transfer, budget, transfer window, team culture, ego, entitlement, asset stripping, directors' loans* – well, I don't want to bore you, but 'Glazers Out!'

What have you learned?

1. **Jot down words or phrases to steal.**
2. **Write down ideas, characters, settings, plots you can use in your own writing.**
3. **Write down anything you have learned about the exam, punctuation, spelling.**
4. **Rewrite part of the answer to give it great grades.**

_____
_____
_____
_____
_____
_____
_____
_____
_____
_____
_____
_____
_____
_____
_____
_____
_____
_____
_____

Response 8

A disturbing fog seeped into the place, smothering it in a duvet of gloom. Only scattering clouds shaded the sun. The coal black trees were company. They gestured to the sky in hateful anger. The fog covered the trees' nakedness, hiding their shame. Again and again, and again, and again, predatory thorns stabbed at man and vegetable. Screams of agony and misery reverberated only to cease like rain and hail.

Again and again, and again, and again. Branches cracked and snapped and whirled and slashed as the gust of hate came barrelling on, as though to hum a song.

"See it," it said.

"See what we have become," they said.

Yet these pleas met with stone hearts, lifeless as the trees.

The gusts spluttered and spluttered, as the day didn't move. The deities mixed their evil brew of thorns and fog. The pot was boiled away some more, and again for a final touch. Suddenly, all was done. A halting stop it was. The silence was as threatening as Genghis Kahn. The calmness was as final as a night-time bath. The trees bowed announcing "Something for everyone." And all things became their panspermia.

A circle of lifelessness. A lifeless circle. A ring of sudden ceasing stood in the foreground. Dressed in dark dust and clothed in fern, it stood like a castle. The entrance was like a drawbridge of death. An outline of swords sprang forward as it swung open by a benign breeze. Again and again, and again, and again. Stab and thrust, until it's over.

257 words

A05 22

Original AO6 15

My Commentary

The examiners have decided that we can pretend that there is such a thing as descriptive writing, that exists on its own, and has different rules to the kind of description we find in real books.

There isn't.

The result is very bad description. Many of the skills which are rewarded in this piece are also examples of how to write very badly.

For example, do you have any clear picture of what has just happened in this text? I bet you don't. I certainly don't. It is just a jumble of imagery, to prove that the student is describing.

Yes, this is a metaphor: "smothering it in a duvet of gloom". And then just to prove that the student can write metaphors, they follow up with two more: "The coal black trees were company. They gestured to the sky in hateful anger." Yes, some personification. But in the rest of the piece, the trees are not company at all, so the description is simply wrong. It doesn't fit.

Here's another example: "The fog covered the trees' nakedness, hiding their shame". This last one is quite amusing, although I don't know if it is supposed to be. Embarrassed trees is a nice idea, but it doesn't fit with hateful anger. So, the description as a whole doesn't make sense.

So, metaphors are excellent. Personification is excellent. But do we really need so many? Not to help us picture the scene. They are mainly there to prove that the student is describing, rather than help us picture a character or setting. And the picture they do describe is confusing, because they contradict the rest of the description.

Then we have a bit of a chorus or a motif, "Again and again, and again, and again" which is ok, but not really interesting enough to be repeated again and again.

Then we have another personification: "predatory thorns stabbed at man and vegetable". Now some dramatic "Screams of agony and misery reverberated only to cease like rain and hail." There is no reason for the screams – invisible people have been introduced into the landscape just so we can have some description of sound. But they are not sounds we would expect to hear. Have you even been in the countryside and paused to listen to people screaming?

You might have heard me screaming reading this answer though.

Suddenly stopping the screams is also not very likely, but it is just there so we can now have a simile. Again, just to prove that there are lots of descriptive techniques.

Now we get a list of verbs, "Branches cracked and snapped and whirled and slashed" which is actually pretty good. But then the wind is described in a metaphor, "as the gust of hate came barrelling on, as though to hum a song." But the two ideas of 'hate' and 'song' really don't belong together, and this makes the simile ridiculous.

The words that the trees speak to the wind are pointless. There are no hearts, so they can't be stone.

The idea of gods stirring weather in a pot, like witches stirring a potion could work, but it isn't really developed here – witches would work better than deities. Adding in only one ingredient, the thorns, makes no sense either.

What was the 'final touch'? There isn't one.

Now we get another list of pointless similes and metaphors which don't help us picture the scene any better, "The silence was as threatening as Genghis Kahn. The calmness was as final as a night-time bath. The trees bowed announcing "Something for everyone." The personification again feels amusing, which I don't think it is meant to be. Calmness and silence don't belong together here – calmness and threat are opposites.

The paragraph ends with a sentence which makes no sense, "And all things became their panspermia." Even when you look up the word 'panspermia', as I had to, it still doesn't make sense.

The final paragraph starts with "A circle of lifelessness. A lifeless circle. A ring of sudden ceasing stood in the foreground." The rhythm of this description is great, especially the sibilance. But there is no circle, or if there is, we have no idea what it is. Trees, a rock formation, a pond, a stone circle? Description can be surprising, but it can't confuse. The reader has to know what you are describing.

The ending is therefore meaningless – we have no idea what swung open, what is being stabbed, what is over. It is simply gibberish described with loads of similes and repetition.

AO5 Content and Organisation

Compelling, Convincing Communication   **22-24 marks**
1. Extensive and ambitious vocabulary
2. Sustained crafting of linguistic devices
3. Varied and inventive use of structural features
4. Fluently linked paragraphs

So, when you look at the bullet points above, the examiners have ignored what is in bold. It isn't convincing, and it isn't compelling. Instead, they have just looked at the bullet points. It certainly does 1, 2 and 3. It can't do 4, because a text that doesn't make sense, can't be "fluently linked".

Anyway, my ring of sudden ceasing stands in the foreground, so I'll stop complaining. You can write crap as long as you use lots and lots of *simile, metaphor, personification, alliteration, sibilance*.

AO6

Level 4: Imaginative and Accurate   **13-16 marks**
- Wide range of punctuation is used with a high level of accuracy
- Uses a full range of appropriate sentence forms for effect
- Uses Standard English consistently and appropriately
- No mistakes with grammar
- Very few mistakes in spelling, including ambitious vocabulary
- Extensive and ambitious use of vocabulary

What have you learned?

1. **Jot down words or phrases to steal.**
2. **Write down ideas, characters, settings, plots you can use in your own writing.**
3. **Write down anything you have learned about the exam, punctuation, spelling.**
4. **Rewrite part of the answer to give it great grades.**

_____

_____

_____

_____

_____

_____

_____

_____

_____

_____

_____

_____

_____

_____

These Answers are Based on Paper 1 June 2019

The Question

Students had the choice to write a story with the title 'Abandoned'. (I have had to change this so I can't be accused of plagiarism).

Or they could write a description of a market suggested by a picture.

Response 1 (Imagine the title is 'Rejection')

Rejection. How do you think it might feel?

Suppose you get out of bed or came in and you had been rejected by everyone you love. Everything you love has vanished. Well, this is the tale of small Jenny.

Jenny was a 16 year old girl. She was enjoying a really happy life until a tragedy took place. She got out of bed and all the people in this tiny village had vanished. She couldn't understand where they were or why they had gone.

She rang everyone she knew, but no joy. She would call and call and call. Jenny was petrified. She was a young lass, not understanding what or why it happened. It simply had.

A05 6

Original AO6 5

My Commentary

AO5

1. We can see that this student's main problem is that they have spent too long thinking and too little writing. Writing is thinking. Just write, and cross out anything that's rubbish.

2. If this is you, you will get much better marks by writing a positive and negative scene in advance and learning them, almost word for word.

3. You will then be able to adapt them to any exam question. Whatever you write will therefore be both longer and better than this.

4. Obviously, a student who writes so little is also a student who leaves out most of the punctuation. I've corrected this. If this is like your writing, you can also make sure the writing you memorise is correctly punctuated, so that you also learn the correct punctuation.

5. But, if this is all you can write, you are also wasting your time in class. You really need to practise writing what comes into your head, then reading it out loud to make sure it makes sense. This will make you a much better writer for life, not just for the exam.

Simple, Limited Communication   **4-6 marks**
   - Simple vocabulary

- Simple linguistic devices
- Simple structure
- Random paragraphs in the wrong order

AO6
Level 2: Sometimes Imaginative and Sometimes Accurate   **5-8 marks**
- Some control of a range of punctuation
- Attempts a variety of sentence forms
- Some use of Standard English
- Some mistakes with tenses or plurals
- Some accurate spelling of more complex words
- Varied vocabulary

What have you learned?

1. **Jot down words or phrases to steal.**
2. **Write down ideas, characters, settings, plots you can use in your own writing.**
3. **Write down anything you have learned about the exam, punctuation, spelling.**
4. **Rewrite part of the answer to give it great grades.**

_____

_____

_____

_____

_____

_____

_____

_____

_____

_____

_____

_____

_____

_____

_____

_____

_____

_____

_____

<u>**Response 2**</u>

Staring, boring, detesting, ruined animals squashed together as if they were a single thing. Dried blood smeared and dripped from the sheep sliced open and hanging from the deathly rafters.

Sunshine peeped in, hoping to bring happiness to the dead stall of the market.

The wives shopped, not looking with her bruised eyes, bent over and chose a stack of grapes that were bunched in ripped bags, *attempting to attack* the shoppers that would pass along **the *arteries* of the market**.

Smelly cheeses sat up hoping to be picked **like auditioning actresses** as the shoppers watched and stopped in their clingy red dress not wanting to breath any dirt in.

Mystery, young and fragile women came in front of the rounded shop assistant who she tries to make small talk with. Her blue un-ironed dress clung tight with her apron which was spattered with blood and uglier than a bull's horn.

Women, men, passed each other as they walked in an atmosphere of quiet. Eyes angled downwards through a scattering of messy death on the ground.

To the left were ripe green bananas **hoping to be bought soon. They crowded together, remaining alert** under the *sagging ceiling*.

Clutching the pig's head firm, the frightening woman in front of the rounded shop assistant fails to lift the *huge hard head* onto the *tight table top*.

Everyone's face was still, **as though they were corpses**. The shopper which had **a forest growing on his head** walked down a row of stalls while dead fish scales caught on his aging skin.

258 words

AO5 9

Original AO6 6

My Commentary

1. The student is doing their best to describe all the sights they can see.

2. But, we can tell that they never read their writing out loud to see if it makes sense. There are too many different ways in which this student doesn't make sense – but reading aloud would cure all of them. This is the biggest weakness which limits the mark to "attempts" rather than "some success".

3. Although there are a lot of similes and metaphors, they often feel random and confusing. This unfortunately means that the good ones appear accidental. They are in bold. Alliteration and sibilance are in italics.

4. The same is true of many of the adjectives.

5. In reality, students who are confusing in what they say are also terrible at punctuation. I have corrected the punctuation here, so that you are not distracted by that.

The student is not yet:

Some Successful Communication   **10-12 marks**

1. Trying to use interesting vocabulary
2. Some use of linguistic devices
3. Some use of structural features
4. Some use of paragraphs

Their skills are:

Attempts

1-4 are attempted but are usually not successful   **7-9 marks**

AO6

Level 2: Sometimes Imaginative and Sometimes Accurate   **5-8 marks**
- Some control of a range of punctuation
- Attempts a variety of sentence forms
- Some use of Standard English
- Some mistakes with tenses or plurals
- Some accurate spelling of more complex words
- Varied vocabulary

What have you learned?

1. **Jot down words or phrases to steal.**
2. **Write down ideas, characters, settings, plots you can use in your own writing.**
3. **Write down anything you have learned about the exam, punctuation, spelling.**
4. **Rewrite part of the answer to give it great grades.**

_____

_____

_____

_____

_____

_____

_____

_____

_____

_____

_____

_____

Response 3

This is no ordinary shopping experience. All day, every day; from dawn till dusk, myriad of people flood the market stalls and make it seem **like it's an invasion of a swarm of locusts**.

However, not all shopping experiences are similar.

Lorries left at shop *fronts filled* with intangible vegetables and *fruits*. The noise attacked me every time I ventured closer and closer: infants wailing with anger, lorries honking near me, and stall holders yelling to shoppers to buy their goods.

Most markets are not the benefit most people imagine them to be. Indeed they are often unsettling places to visit. *Some stalls* hang up and *sell slaughtered* animals. Fish are raw, and smell vile, particularly in the heat. They are rather unsettling as you can *smell the scent* of rotting meat; *flies* landing on these *fleshy* animals and buzzing about.

The vile scent of rotting flesh enclosed each shopper, and made them suffering. Ghastly.

The gory location, which was jam-packed with shoppers made it seem like a horror film for youngsters as children tend to wander and go missing.

180 words

A05 12

Original AO6 9

My Commentary

AO5

1. This is typical of a student who can get a higher mark, but throws it away with some obvious errors. Reading this out loud (in their head – it is an exam after all) would have saved them from these:

   - Switching between the present and past tense.
   - Unnecessary repetition.
   - Not finishing sentences towards the end of the piece, because the student hasn't realised sentences containing verbs ending in 'ing' need to have a verb which completes in action.
   - The last two lines don't make sense.
   - The student is trying to use vocabulary which is too advanced for them, rather than say exactly what they mean. See for example: 'myriad of', 'intangible', 'fleshy', 'enclosed'.
   - The student is starting to vary the length of sentences, and to start most of them with a different word. However, 3 still begin with 'the'. This would be ok if there were more sentences, in a longer piece.

2. It is too short to be consistent, especially as there are a few inconsistencies – the errors pointed out above.

3. A lot of the time, the student is trying to *explain* what the market is like, rather than *show* it. The easiest way around that would be to introduce a character, and make them observe the market place as they move through it.

4. There are no metaphors and only one simile. The student is not really thinking about the sound either, so there is very little alliteration or sibilance. What is used seems as though it may have been accidental rather than planned.

The student is not yet:
Clear   **13-15 marks**

The answer is still:
Some Successful Communication   **10-12 marks**
- Trying to use interesting vocabulary
- Some use of linguistic devices
- Some use of structural features
- Some use of paragraphs

AO6

Level 3: Usually Imaginative and Usually Accurate   **9-12 marks**
- Uses a variety of sentence forms for effect
- Mostly uses Standard English appropriately
- Few mistakes in grammar
- Increasingly sophisticated use of vocabulary

What have you learned?

1. Jot down words or phrases to steal.
2. Write down ideas, characters, settings, plots you can use in your own writing.
3. Write down anything you have learned about the exam, punctuation, spelling.
4. Rewrite part of the answer to give it great grades.

_____

_____

_____

_____

_____

_____

_____

_____

_____

_____

_____

_____

_____

_____

Response 4

Deserted. Silence echoes through the dark empty hallways. People sat behind massive metal gates. The sounds of doors clanking night and day. As the policeman with the dark reinforced vest and many steel tools crammed onto his belt left and slammed the doors. I felt fear inside as I told myself, "how will I ever see daylight from inside this cell again?"

I looked over my cell … narrow steel bars blurred my rectangular window, a bunk which looked like it had been there for centuries. A wall decorated with a cracked mirror. It had patches of mud all over. My faced dripped in sweat. I was on my own. Left with no opportunity to tell my story.

My brown beard spiked up. I shut my eyes and pictured if I chose a different path and what it would be like. Tears shedded along my cheeks. All my feelings cried out, like a stream flowing down a river. Powerless, I sat on the bunk which felt like a giant concrete slab. Hoping the earth would swallow me any time soon.

I looked up … hoping this was all a horrifying, nightmarish trauma. I was wrong. The lumpy brown walls felt as though they were trapping me. I tried to scream. No sound came out. The clanking of doors still sounding through my head. Why was I locked up? Why?

I just sat there, miserable. Sorrow was visible everywhere on me. There was no escape. "How could I do it!" I kept asking myself again and again. The feel of scrubbing so hard at the blood which covered my hand. It wouldn't go away.

If I could turn back time things would be so different. But I couldn't. I couldn't go back. Locked up forever. I rolled over. I lay down without a sound and slept. Twisting and squirming separately all through. "Help! Help!" I yelled. Woke up fast and leaped up onto the dusty banana yellow floor.

327 words

A05 14

Original AO6 9

My Commentary

AO5

This student is doing their best at following their teacher's instructions.

1. They are making sure to include the senses, especially sound.

2. They are trying to use lots of adjectives.

3. They know they have to vary long and short sentences.

4. They understand that including a character's feelings will help the description feel as though it can fit in a novel.

But, there are some very typical mistakes which lots of students like this have. For example:

1. They don't realise that if your first verb in a sentence ends in 'ing', you need to have another verb later which completes an action. Without a competed action, your sentence won't make sense.

2. They don't have a very wide vocabulary, so they don't always use it in the right way, and they make up 'shedded'.

3. Some of the adjectives are just there to use an adjective, rather than help us picture the scene, like the lumpy wall and the banana yellow floor.

4. Many of the sentences start with the same word, so they feel boring and predictable.

Consistent, Clear Communication   **16-18 marks**
1. Increasingly sophisticated vocabulary
2. A range of successful linguistic devices
3. Effective use of structural features
4. Paragraphs which make sense in the right order

Clear   **13-15 marks**
1-4 above, but not always consistent

AO6

Level 3: Usually Imaginative and Usually Accurate   **9-12 marks**
- Uses a variety of sentence forms for effect
- Mostly uses Standard English appropriately
- Few mistakes in grammar
- Increasingly sophisticated use of vocabulary

What have you learned?

1. **Jot down words or phrases to steal.**
2. **Write down ideas, characters, settings, plots you can use in your own writing.**
3. **Write down anything you have learned about the exam, punctuation, spelling.**
4. **Rewrite part of the answer to give it great grades.**

_____

_____

_____

_____

_____

_____

_____

_____

_____

Response 5

The market place is lively with bustle. This tiny corner of the world is a rainbow of colours. Colourful produce glows from every stall and *counter: there are crabs, there are carrots*, there are many types of meat, there are vegetables and fruit and there are cured meats and cheeses. Baskets and trays hang from wooden beams, in a display of green. **Colour explodes everywhere, like a fountain of sherbet**, yet each stall is tidily organised. It's **as vibrant as a party**: it's as though **each stall is a drunken guest screeching with excitement**.

Fluorescent lights flicker from the beams; strobing the bustling alleys of stalls. The heavy canopy (suspended from these joists) protects the market from the boring world outside.

Shoppers are carrying bags of various colours from the various stalls – many are orange, many are red.

The fish seller on one side of the row of stalls is clutching a fish's head whose eyes *are as large as saucers*. On the other side is the butcher, *slicing a strip of fresh* meat. A huge flank – in the process of carving – *dangles* from a *beam, demanding* to be seen. *Beneath* it are numerous fruits and stacks of eggs. At the rear is a grocer who is displaying fresh vegetables. There are potatoes, cauliflowers, sprouts – every vegetable for sale in this market place!

I picture the customers and stall holders haggling for a great price and how the noisy environment causes a hot environment.

Yet, this market place is filled only with adults. Could this vanish one day? Could this tiny paradise, filled with happiness, gradually vanish?

267 words

A05 15

Original AO6 10

My Commentary

AO5

1. This student is writing in clear sentences and paragraphs.

2. Although most of the paragraphs could be put in any order and still make the same sense, the student has at least thought about the best ways to start and finish. This means that the structure is not well crafted yet.

3. The student has tried to use different vocabulary to bring the scene to life. None of the words are just there to show off. Instead, they help us picture the scene. Occasionally the same word is used more than once, which makes the description a bit repetitive.

4. The similes and metaphors also work. Again, they aren't just there to prove that the student knows how to write a simile and a metaphor. They help us picture the scene. But, there aren't enough of them to show that there is a good range.

5. The student has attempted quite a few types of sentences, including lists. Often these are a bit predictable and repetitive. However, the variety of subordinate clauses means that overall the sentences are successful.

Consistent, Clear Communication   **16-18 marks**
1. Increasingly sophisticated vocabulary
2. A range of successful linguistic devices
3. Effective use of structural features
4. Paragraphs which make sense in the right order

Clear   **13-15 marks**
1-4 above, but not always consistent

AO6

Level 3: Usually Imaginative and Usually Accurate **9-12 marks**
1. Uses a variety of sentence forms for effect
2. Mostly uses Standard English appropriately
3. Few mistakes in grammar
4. Increasingly sophisticated use of vocabulary

The student has attempted to use a range of punctuation. The dash is used correctly, and the colon has been used correctly both to introduce a list and an explanation.

What have you learned?

1. Jot down words or phrases to steal.
2. Write down ideas, characters, settings, plots you can use in your own writing.
3. Write down anything you have learned about the exam, punctuation, spelling.
4. Rewrite part of the answer to give it great grades.

_____

_____

_____

_____

_____

_____

_____

_____

_____

_____

_____

_____

_____

<u>**Response 6**</u>

The night was silent, apart from the gentle rumble of traffic in the distance together with the sounds of *concrete hit by cold* rain. And of course the rumbling in her belly. The car park appeared empty and around it was a barbed fence **as tall as the trees**.

Her reddened cheeks were stung red by the pelting rain. Her blond *cascading curls were crushed* by the yellow hood of her coat. Surely her mother would soon come, in the green Volvo, alarmingly desperate to rescue her. Any time now.

The unpleasantness of waiting in the rain coupled with the fear in her chest and the deep hollow in her belly made her heart race.

Just then she saw a flash of green within the black spreading darkness that seemed to envelope her. Was that her?

No, the colour vanished and she was abandoned once more. Soaked. Still waiting outside school.

She was drawn to look down at her boots. Thankfully they were her best waterproofs, neony orange with roses tattooed in the sides. Her mum hadn't stopped her from buying them when she left reception class. She loved them deeply.

Splash. She dipped the tip of her toes and tapped a puddle. Splash. She jumped. The *puddles pooling* in the car park were suddenly inviting. Carefully, she hopped in on her right foot. Then the left. Right. Suddenly, she leapt, *landing two footed in a deeper puddle*. Water *soared, soaking* her dull grey uniform and she shrieked at the *feeling of frozen water. Freezing*, she stopped.

Well, it *beat sitting* on the *curb, sulking impatiently.*

Leap after leap, she jumped; nothing would put her off. Each splash triggered her laughter as she stomped through the wet, engrossed, by the empty school.

"Jessica!"

She suddenly stopped, nearly falling into a puddle. The green Volvo was waiting and her mum looked anxious and sorry.

Smiling with joy, Jessica sprang towards her mother, ready to share everything about her school day.

329 words

A05 19

Original AO6 14

My Commentary

AO5

1. This answer is typical of a student who is making sudden breakthroughs in their writing. You can see this because nearly every description helps us. The detail about the yellow hood doesn't: it feels as though it is just to cram in an extra adjective.

2. The sentences are varied in length and structure, and the sequence describing splashing in the puddles uses one word sentences in a way which helps us imagine Jessica's actions. They aren't just there because the student has randomly decided to put in a one word sentence anywhere.

3. Most sentences start with a different word.

4. There is a lot of sibilance and alliteration to help us hear and picture the scene.

5. The description feels real because we get the character's feelings, which means it could easily fit in a novel. Real writers describe this way.

6. It starts with a very boring simile, and that is the only simile or metaphor in the whole piece. This is sadly a major reason why it doesn't get more marks. Don't overload your writing with similes though – metaphors are even better and are usually more original.

7. The student has picked a very ordinary scene. This is often a good tactic, as it stops the writing turning into horror, killing, stabbing, slashing or containing lots of over-exaggerated misery. But, it does mean that you have to work hard on the vocabulary and linguistic devices in order to make it compelling and convincing. That's where this student could improve.

AO5 Content and Organisation

Compelling, Convincing Communication   **22-24 marks**
   1. Extensive and ambitious vocabulary
   2. Sustained crafting of linguistic devices
   3. Varied and inventive use of structural features
   4. Fluently linked paragraphs

Convincing   **19–21 marks**
1-4 above, but not inventive and compelling

AO6

Level 4: Imaginative and Accurate   **13-16 marks**
   1. Wide range of punctuation is used with a high level of accuracy
   2. Uses a full range of appropriate sentence forms for effect
   3. Uses Standard English consistently and appropriately
   4. No mistakes with grammar
   5. Very few mistakes in spelling, including ambitious vocabulary
   6. Extensive and ambitious use of vocabulary

<u>**Response 7**</u>

There's a heartbeat to every city centre. In every town **there beats a communal heart**, and this town was no different. Scores of ornately cluttered, overstuffed stalls spread in columns, flooding the streets with colours and smells.

Customers hopped curiously from one stall to the next, side by side, but totally separated in style and goods. Grocers, butchers, fish merchants all part of the hustle and bustle of stall holders' sales pitches: a *chaotic and crowded* scene, yet welcoming and seductive. Within **this battleground** community somehow flourished.

On one side, succulent fruits piled improbably on top of each other, **tugging and calling at the passers by, daring them** to part with their coin. On the other *side, a side of pork, sliced* and hung from the rafters alongside game birds, choice cuts of steak, as fresh as the butches could make them.

The dangling pig acted as sentinel, **guarding the range of meats** and poultry *spread across the stalls*. It stood out here, as did everything else.

Down one street, *busy and bustling* with people, excited voices filled the pavements. Cheeses, garlics, onions and peppers all **battled** in the powerful summer heat, competed with the perfume of vibrant roses and stunning flowers on the stall next door, attracting customers. They felt as one with nature. A scent of lobster and crab recreated a memory of the seas, and fought off the delicious swirling aroma from bakeries.

The customers were *similarly* energised. *Sellers* with a *mastery of salesmanship enticed* their public with enticing bargains and beckoning smiles promising a deal. Young children watched open mouthed as they tried to choose between ice *cream and candy* as a weekend treat. **Palms were greased with coin**, and the exchanges made everyone feel they had won a prize.

This heart beat was essential, the centre of the town, and this length of street with *flowers, foods and fruits* was worth more than money or profit.

321 words

A05 22

AO6 13

My Commentary

AO5

1. It has all the usual stuff – lists, vocabulary choices, lots of adjectives, quite a lot of metaphor and a bit of simile, alliteration and sibilance. There's at least one in every sentence – that is what 'a range' means at the top level.

2. Lists, with clauses, or noun phrases, really do help you write a great description.

3. The student focuses on colour, sound and smell in ways which feel helpful to picturing the scene – none of these feel artificial or forced. They would fit in a novel.

4. The student is consciously trying to start each sentence in a different way, with a different word.
5. The writing is structured around simple contrasts – on one side, on the other side; candy and ice cream, etc.

6. The examiner loves the idea of a circular structure, so starting and finishing with the same metaphor is a winner. In this examiner's mind, this will make it convincing and compelling.

Compelling, Convincing Communication   **22-24 marks**
1. Extensive and ambitious vocabulary
2. Sustained crafting of linguistic devices
3. Varied and inventive use of structural features
4. Fluently linked paragraphs

AO6

Level 4: Imaginative and Accurate   **13-16 marks**
1. Wide range of punctuation is used with a high level of accuracy
2. Uses a full range of appropriate sentence forms for effect
3. Uses Standard English consistently and appropriately
4. No mistakes with grammar
5. Very few mistakes in spelling, including ambitious vocabulary
6. Extensive and ambitious use of vocabulary

You can see the main one holding this back (in the examiner's mind) is the lack of variety in punctuation. Colon, exclamation mark, ellipsis, brackets, dashes – you remember! Not even a question mark. The examiner is fuming!

What have you learned?

1. **Jot down words or phrases to steal.**
2. **Write down ideas, characters, settings, plots you can use in your own writing.**
3. **Write down anything you have learned about the exam, punctuation, spelling.**
4. **Rewrite part of the answer to give it great grades.**

_____

_____

_____

_____

_____

_____

_____

_____

_____

_____

Response 8

Max waited on the *bench beneath* the oak trees and red squirrels he had been watching in his last weeks here. The bench was not the apex of comfort he had imagined spending his days on; its creaking spars **filling the emptiness inside him**. Yet, he was quite used to it now and his *sole* antidote to the *sad*, redundant, *harsh loveless* day.

He had been sitting for ours. Max *fumbled into the folds* of his pocket and drew out the mobile his son had pressed on him, hoping to fill **his increasingly empty life**.

"Soon," he wondered, "soon she'll send me a word," but yet again as he fumbled through recent messages from the enchanting woman whose smiles had promised so much …

Emptiness

Max was puzzled; he had imagined that old age taught wisdom in knowing whom to trust. She had seemed so perfect from the start. With a mood of delight and optimism trailing them everywhere their bond had been deep. After confiding in each other for hours, they had arranged to meet again and he'd determinedly made sure that he could be summoned at any time to have his *future filled* once more with her company. He had never looked too *far into the future* but, the moment he got here, he was confronted by the same sense he was feeling now.

Emptiness

As he sank into the bench and mulled over the last three days (**like a film rewinding in his head**) Max understood there would be no second chance. No bright future. No joy to cherish.

Emptiness

Max **sank into remembrance** as he *drifted, despondent* on his *bench, a building which was bathed in blackness* with the *setting of the sun.*

Abandoned.

288 words

AO5 24

Original AO6 15

My Commentary

AO5

1. Once again, the top marks are earned by a story rather than a description.

2. The student loses a couple of marks because the writing doesn't feel fully controlled – there is too little detail of the woman and their previous encounters for us to work out how why she was initially so kind to him, and why she has now refused to show up.

3. You can see that the student is trying to vary sentences for effect. The repetition of a single word sentence is a little gimmicky, but here it works like a chorus.

4. The description of the place mimics Max's mood and thoughts. You'll remember that this is pathetic fallacy, and makes the description worthwhile – it is also telling us about Max, rather than just simply describing the scene.

5. Examiners like flashback. It is a useful technique in order to turn a description into a story if you need to. It is also useful because it gives us the character's thoughts, which gives us a much more detailed picture of them.

Compelling, Convincing Communication   **22-24 marks**
- Extensive and ambitious vocabulary
- Sustained crafting of linguistic devices
- Varied and inventive use of structural features
- Fluently linked paragraphs

AO6

Level 4: Imaginative and Accurate   **13-16 marks**
- Wide range of punctuation is used with a high level of accuracy
- Uses a full range of appropriate sentence forms for effect
- Uses Standard English consistently and appropriately
- No mistakes with grammar
- Very few mistakes in spelling, including ambitious vocabulary
- Extensive and ambitious use of vocabulary

What have you learned?

1. **Jot down words or phrases to steal.**
2. **Write down ideas, characters, settings, plots you can use in your own writing.**
3. **Write down anything you have learned about the exam, punctuation, spelling.**
4. **Rewrite part of the answer to give it great grades.**

_____

_____

_____

_____

_____

_____

_____

_____

_____

_____

_____

_____

Here's my full mark answer to this question

The Market Place

The artist might have waited for just this moment. A man, a woman, a narrow path between stalls selling violence and carnage. The man looks predatory, his eyes in shadow and wearing what looks like a turtle neck jumper and a leather jacket. He blocks her path. The artist was probably a woman, because she sees her subject try to alter her path. She steps away from the swordfish, the parade of decapitated heads thrusting their blades into the air. But to her right hangs the flayed carcass of a pig, it's shiny muscles and sinews stripped of flesh and glistening. Perhaps this is the lesser of two evils. Behind the pig, a butcher sculpts its flank with a knife, like an artist. To her left the fish monger grabs hold of a fish-head's sword in a manner than can only be calculated to disgust her.

The scene looks French if the cheeses are anything to go by, and so we'll call the trapped woman trying to change direction Bernadette. Turtle-neck-leather man looks like a poser, the only person in the scene wearing more than shirt sleeves. He must love that jacket in this heat. We'll call him jacket man, Jacque for short.

Bernadette is not dressed to attract attention, not from the back anyway. Her waist looks like it is starting to thicken, though no one could call her fat. Coming up to middle age perhaps. The two small bags she's carrying might mean she lives alone, shopping for one, or the market may be a daily ritual. The artist hasn't cropped the scene too tightly. She wants us to revel in the colours, as well as the blood-red of meat. Bernadette has passed boxes of red peppers crowding the scene with the blush of pink lobsters, and these jostle against the sheaths of green vegetables. Unlike the meat, they seem to lack a form or an identity. We can't tell if one box displays cauliflower or artichokes, and jammed next to it could be leeks or courgettes or even cobs of corn still in their green leaf sleeves.

So Jacque is drawn to the meat, and we wonder, is Bernadette just another kind of meat to him? Has he blocked the path to make her struggle to squeeze past him, for the thrill of it, exercising his power, telling himself perhaps that she would enjoy the forced contact as much as him? We are all animals after all, he might be thinking, standing among the carcasses.

Behind Jacque, and Bernadette can see this, three women are shopping. They might be a comfort to her, safety in numbers. But Jacque has passed them, and none of them have turned to glance at him. He might be harmless, after all. Their eyes are all downcast, focusing on the richness of the stalls, the competing aromas sending their hands into the purses, stroking coins, pondering which flavours to spend on. So perhaps Jacque is not a threat.

Perhaps it is she who has been waiting, waiting by the meat. Notice that her left arm is bent at the elbow, forearm in front of her. She makes as if to fend him off, but what of the fat pockets of his jacket? To brush past him in this narrow path must involve a collision, there is no way out of it now. The artist makes us wonder about the front of the dress. Jacques eyes are also cast down at it. Cleavage. Meat. A suitable distraction.

Yes, that's it. She has waited for such a man. Her arm will meet him while his gaze is hypnotised. Her fingers will be quick, plucking his wallet from him with practiced ease.

623 words

Here is the same description, shortened in case you are a slow writer, but it still scores 100%

The Market Place

The artist might have waited for just this moment. A man, a woman, a narrow path between stalls *selling violence* **and carnage**. The man looks predatory, his eyes in shadow and *wearing what looks like* a turtle neck jumper and a leather jacket. He blocks her path. The artist was probably a woman, because *she sees her subject* try to alter her path. *She steps away from the swordfish*, **the parade of decapitated heads thrusting their blades into the air.** But to her right hangs the flayed carcass of a pig, *it's shiny muscles and sinews stripped of flesh and glistening*. Perhaps *this is the lesser of two evils*. Behind the pig, **a butcher sculpts its flank with a knife, like an artist**. To her left the fish monger grabs hold of a fish-head's sword in a manner than *can only be calculated* to disgust her.

The scene looks French if the cheeses are anything to go by, and so we'll call the trapped woman trying to change direction Bernadette. Turtle-neck-leather man looks like a poser, the only person in the scene wearing more than shirt sleeves. He must love that jacket in this heat. We'll call him jacket man, Jacque for short.

Bernadette is not dressed to attract attention, not from the back anyway. Her waist looks like it is starting to thicken, though no one could call her fat. Coming up to middle age perhaps. The artist wants us to revel in the colours, as well as the blood-red of meat. Boxes of red peppers crowding the scene with the blush of pink lobsters, and **these jostle against the sheaths of green vegetables**.

Jacque is drawn to the meat, and we wonder, is Bernadette just another kind of meat to him? Has he blocked the path to make her *struggle to squeeze* past him, for the thrill of it, exercising his power, telling himself perhaps that she would enjoy the forced contact as much as him? We are all animals after all, he might be thinking, standing among the carcasses.

Perhaps it is she *who has been waiting, waiting* by the meat. Notice that her left arm is bent at the elbow, *forearm in front* of her. She makes as *if to fend* him *off*, **but what of the *fat* pockets of his jacket?** To brush *past* him in this narrow *path* must involve a collision, there is no way out of it now. The artist makes us wonder about the front of the dress. Jacques eyes are also cast down at it. **Cleavage. Meat.** A suitable distraction.

Yes, that's it. She has waited for such a man. Her arm will meet him while his gaze is hypnotised. Her fingers will be quick, *plucking* his wallet from him with *practiced* ease.

469 words

My Commentary

AO5

I wrote this to try to show my students a brilliant trick with the picture question:

Imagine the photograph or picture is produced by an artist, and you are viewing it in a gallery.

- This allows you not just to describe what is in it, but also wonder about the artist's intentions.
- This gives you a really easy way in to writing about characters from a different point of view – and of course it means your description will always be 'inventive and compelling'.

Then I just need to use the **big five**, and make sure they fit with everything else in the description. I've placed simile, metaphor and personification in bold and alliteration and sibilance in italics.

Notice that I have tried to start most sentences with a different word, and I've varied the vocabulary.

AO6

Looking back, I'm a little worried. What will the examiner think about my punctuation?

Examiner: "Sorry, Mr Salles, you haven't used a large enough range of punctuation."

Mr Salles: "It has exactly the right punctuation for its meaning."

Examiner: "Ah, but this is an exam. How do I know that you understand how to use a colon and an exclamation mark if you don't show me? How do I know you can use brackets, or an ellipsis?"

Mr Salles: "I see. You could just give me a few sentences and tell me to put those pieces of punctuation in. Test me that way. And then I could learn to be a real writer, instead of pointlessly putting in punctuation where it is not needed."

Examiner: "Look, our job at AQA is to help you reach your potential, which we define as getting a grade. We don't care whether you are actually any good at writing. I mean, who writes 500 word descriptions? No one in the real world. But it is our way of helping you reach your potential. Now, do you want the marks or not?"

Mr Salles: "%$?@!"

Ok, let's get the marks

Colon: The man looks predatory: his eyes in shadow and *wearing what looks like* a turtle neck jumper and a leather jacket.

Ellipsis: Perhaps it is she *who has been waiting … waiting* by the meat.

Brackets: Her waist looks like it is starting to thicken (though no one could call her fat).

Exclamation mark: Yes, that's it!

There you go. This is a range of punctuation. My work on for the exam will be to practise putting in punctuation, whether I need it or not.

What have you learned?

1. Jot down words or phrases to steal.
2. Write down ideas, characters, settings, plots you can use in your own writing.
3. Write down anything you have learned about the exam, punctuation, spelling.
4. Rewrite part of the answer to give it great grades.

_____

_____

_____

_____

_____

_____

_____

_____

_____

_____

_____

_____

_____

_____

_____

_____

_____

_____

_____

_____

_____

_____

_____

_____

_____

_____

_____

Based Paper 1 November 2018

The Question

Students were given the choice to write a story about time travel based on a picture. The picture was back and white, and appeared to be the interior of a railway station.

Or they could write a description of life in 200 years' time. (This resulted in lots of description which felt a lot more like an explanation).

Response 1

Screaming streams of sunlight **exploded** through the *stained glass windows and splattered* the floor from above. A light filled stage dancing with shadows which wandered by. I ambled on, free from any worries. My shadow reflected my carefree mood. It entered the stage *like a leaping tiger*, spinning *in an elegant waltz*. Beneath it all, I was petrified.

This was my first experience of time travel. I became eligible at the age of 21. Time travel was only legal from this birthday. Apparently, age helps your body to transport. Yet that wasn't the real reason. After 21 you are deemed to have lived enough of life so not returning is no tragedy.

112 words

AO5 8

Original AO6 8

My Commentary

AO5

1. Although it starts confidently with sibilance, contains a simile and a metaphor, it is just too short to score well.

2. It also swaps between the present and the past tenses, which shows a lack of control.

3. But, look how easy it is to gain marks with almost no work or words!

Some Successful Communication	10-12 marks
1. Trying to use interesting vocabulary	
2. Some use of linguistic devices	
3. Some use of structural features	
4. Some use of paragraphs	

Attempts	
1-4 above are attempted but are usually not successful	**7-9 marks**

AO6

Level 2: Sometimes Imaginative and Sometimes Accurate	5-8 marks
1. Some control of a range of punctuation	
2. Attempts a variety of sentence forms	

3. Some use of Standard English
4. Some mistakes with tenses or plurals
5. Some accurate spelling of more complex words
6. Varied vocabulary

What have you learned?

1. **Jot down words or phrases to steal.**
2. **Write down ideas, characters, settings, plots you can use in your own writing.**
3. **Write down anything you have learned about the exam, punctuation, spelling.**
4. **Rewrite part of the answer to give it great grades.**

_____

_____

_____

_____

_____

_____

_____

_____

_____

_____

_____

_____

_____

_____

_____

_____

_____

_____

_____

_____

_____

_____

_____

_____

_____

<u>Response 2</u>

It is an ordinary day for Dan. The earth was ending. Just the noise of floating transport and the *searing sun* baking each clod of mud. *Crimson shades spread across the sky*. From the terrifying and wicked sun.

Dan is preparing, dressing in his hazard clothes which is now viewed as normal to them, because it is created to keep out the sun. It stops him getting hot and keeps the sun away from his flesh as **it would turn his skin to toast**. Going outside, he must also wear headgear made to make the sky appear dark. Every person has to wear these to prevent death in the world they exist in now.

250 years ago the earth was perfect. It had plants, animals, available water! Looks as though life was perfect. Today, you own stunning modern stuff like floating transport and so on, but now each day we struggle to survive by hunting water sources and preventing the sun touching us. There has been not a single drop of water from clouds in 200 years!

177 words

AO5 11

Original AO6 9

My Commentary

AO5

1. This is clearly a worse writer, especially with the change from present to past tense.

2. Yet it is longer, so it is more developed.

3. It has a greater range of punctuation.

4. It uses contrast, especially between then and now.

5. The student is trying to start sentences with different words.

6. But there is only one weak simile, and very little alliteration or sibilance.

Some Successful Communication   **10-12 marks**
  - Trying to use interesting vocabulary
  - Some use of linguistic devices
  - Some use of structural features
  - Some use of paragraphs

AO6

Level 3: Usually Imaginative and Usually Accurate   **9-12 marks**
  - A range of punctuation is used, mostly accurate
  - Uses a variety of sentence forms for effect
  - Mostly uses Standard English appropriately
  - Few mistakes in grammar
  - Mostly accurate spelling, including complex and irregular words

- Increasingly sophisticated use of vocabulary, which you remember counts twice, as it appears in AO5

What have you learned?

1. Jot down words or phrases to steal.
2. Write down ideas, characters, settings, plots you can use in your own writing.
3. Write down anything you have learned about the exam, punctuation, spelling.
4. Rewrite part of the answer to give it great grades.

_____

_____

_____

_____

_____

_____

_____

_____

_____

_____

_____

_____

_____

_____

_____

_____

_____

_____

_____

_____

_____

_____

_____

_____

_____

_____

_____

_____

Response 3

Living in 250 years from now will be totally different. Man's existence is about to *cease. Society is not in chaos*, however. *Society is strengthened by science*. Artificial intelligence and computers got so clever. Robots conquered us. They defeated us humans. Roads no longer have sidewalks, just a hard black coating with what seem like metal *tracks traced* into every street. That was the way they spread. Just the most wealthy robots had a human being as a pet, hovering at their sides, trapped in a clear glass square, **like a floating prison**. Each road had a D. D. T. – digital, dematerializing, transporter. They would stroll in one and abracadabra, dematerialize into the ether, transporting them to where they wanted to be.

Stores are unusual, because they had no need of food or drink. They didn't have clothes. They just used upgrade shops and pet shops. There you would buy what your human pet required.

We worried that humans had destroyed the earth but really we only ruined ourselves so robots could flourish.

173 words

AO5 13

Original AO6 9

My Commentary

AO5

1. There are hardly any mistakes in tense.

2. There is only one simile or metaphor (which is a problem with the question).

3. There is more regular alliteration, but because of the lack of 2 above, the examiner won't be sure if it is deliberate or a happy accident.

4. The student uses more complex sentence structures. The easiest way to do that is to start most sentences with a different word. That also gives it the sentence variety rewarded in AO6.

5. It uses contrast to create a sense of tension.

6. Vocabulary is starting to be ambitious.

7. The piece is not long enough to show that it is "consistent".

Consistent, Clear Communication	**16-18 marks**
1. Increasingly sophisticated vocabulary	
2. A range of successful linguistic devices	
3. Effective use of structural features	
4. Paragraphs which make sense in the right order	

Clear	**13-15 marks**
1-4 above, but not always consistent	

AO6

Level 3: Usually Imaginative and Usually Accurate   **9-12 marks**

1. A range of punctuation is used, mostly accurate
2. Uses a variety of sentence forms for effect
3. Mostly uses Standard English appropriately
4. Few mistakes in grammar
5. Mostly accurate spelling, including complex and irregular words
6. Increasingly sophisticated use of vocabulary

What have you learned?

1. **Jot down words or phrases to steal.**
2. **Write down ideas, characters, settings, plots you can use in your own writing.**
3. **Write down anything you have learned about the exam, punctuation, spelling.**
4. **Rewrite part of the answer to give it great grades.**

_____

_____

_____

_____

_____

_____

_____

_____

_____

_____

_____

_____

_____

_____

_____

_____

_____

_____

_____

_____

_____

_____

Response 4

Floating airships and 3D projections. That's what we'll experience, dear reader. I can see **cities like computer games**, *filled with floating* roads, threading and spinning between sky towers. Moreover, cars will look like Porsches and Maclarens, and these will be viewed as dull. In two centuries the world will be transformed.

Science will, as it does now, control everything. *Students in schools* won't bother to write, but learn to type, and each will store their workings on a device. Because, now we consider it, *today's tablets* will be made by other brands than IOS and Google.

Receiving a phone call, to find a caller in 3D, as if they've leaped out of your phone to have a gossip, and at the end they vanish. Shazam. **As instant as a blink**.

Nevertheless, although all this technology across most countries, and ignoring its clear flaws, appears fantastic, I also picture a different reality, a reality where the poor are abandoned, ignored, *while wealthy* countries *expand and progress* is real. The poorer *countries will come* last, **like a wrestling match** *where the weakest competitor can't win*.

This is how to imagine the future in 300 years, yet it's one of two pictures. Beside it is a more pleasant image, where the poor aren't asked to wrestle. A future where all nations are equal and prosperity is shared.

224 words

AO5 15

Original AO6 11

My Commentary

AO5

1. Well, there is an obvious increase in length, so it is more sustained. But it is not long enough to called "consistent".

2. There is a lot more metaphor and simile, in bold.

3. Contrast is everywhere.

4. Sentences start in different ways, with different words.

5. There is more sentence variety – both long and complex, and short for impact.

6. Vocabulary is often chosen carefully, with verbs in particular being well chosen.

7. Alliteration and sibilance are being used to emphasise words and ideas.

8. It uses words containing abstract ideas – prosperity, progress, technology, which lead to complex ideas and sophisticated vocabulary.

Consistent, Clear Communication	**16-18 marks**

1. Increasingly sophisticated vocabulary

2. A range of successful linguistic devices
3. Effective use of structural features
4. Paragraphs which make sense in the right order

Clear   **13-15 marks**
1-4 above, but not always consistent

AO6

Level 3: Usually Imaginative and Usually Accurate   **9-12 marks**
- A range of punctuation is used, mostly accurate
- Uses a variety of sentence forms for effect
- Mostly uses Standard English appropriately
- Few mistakes in grammar
- Mostly accurate spelling, including complex and irregular words
- Increasingly sophisticated use of vocabulary

What have you learned?

1. **Jot down words or phrases to steal.**
2. **Write down ideas, characters, settings, plots you can use in your own writing.**
3. **Write down anything you have learned about the exam, punctuation, spelling.**
4. **Rewrite part of the answer to give it great grades.**

_____

_____

_____

_____

_____

_____

_____

_____

_____

_____

_____

_____

_____

_____

_____

_____

_____

_____

_____

Response 5

In 300 years, we should witness great advances in healthcare everywhere in the world, because we might thereby save humanity. *We might also witness* the homeless saved from the *world's* streets with free accommodation. We must hope that *future food shortages, famines and social* disasters will be prevented, and that happiness is *everyone's experience* of life.

In 300 years, the world should be *crime free* and governments be *corruption free*. We hope that racism and sexism, homophobia and all discrimination will be in the past. We hope that in 300 years **lives will be free** and uncontrolled.

*We want a world **free from conflict*** and *people will oppose* each other reasonably, without violence. Violence must be punished instantly. We *all live our lives* by a moral code. **This guides us to our homes** and, believe me, **we all try to find our way home**. Ask no one about their religion and protect those who are criticised for theirs.

We hope *for a future* with *no need for armies as nations will no* longer start wars. We will be saved from *tyrannical dictators, terrorists and armed citizens*, and the vulnerable will no longer be exploited as weak.

We hope in the future that we will no longer turn to drugs in order to find a good life.

216 words

AO5 17

Original AO6 10

My Commentary

AO5

1. You can see that this is identical to a persuasive piece of writing for question 5 of paper 2.

2. It works, because in order to persuade us of what the future should be like, the student has had to describe it. It isn't quite what the examiner expected, but really, it should have been obvious that students would explain and persuade rather than purely describe. Just look at the question.

3. This has meant that there are very few metaphors, although there are just enough for a range.

4. The student is starting sentences with the same words, but this is done for effect. The repetition is drumming home the message that the future needs to be an improvement on the present.

5. The writing contains a range of techniques, especially alliteration, even though we were expecting simile and metaphor instead.

6. Triplets are used repeatedly, as are lists. Although they are traditionally used for persuasive writing, they are still "linguistic devices", so they still count towards the grade.

7. Verbs are beginning to be chosen for their precision and power – e.g. witness, save, prevent, punished, exploited.

8. Emotive language is used frequently, both to highlight the negative of the present and the optimism of the future.

9. Abstract nouns mean that communication is clear, and vocabulary is varied – healthcare, humanity, happiness (and that's just the Hs!)

Consistent, Clear Communication   **16-18 marks**
1. Increasingly sophisticated vocabulary
2. A range of successful linguistic devices
3. Effective use of structural features
4. Paragraphs which make sense in the right order

AO6

Level 3: Usually Imaginative and Usually Accurate   **9-12 marks**
1. A range of punctuation is used, mostly accurate
2. Uses a variety of sentence forms for effect
3. Mostly uses Standard English appropriately
4. Few mistakes in grammar
5. Mostly accurate spelling, including complex and irregular words
6. Increasingly sophisticated use of vocabulary

What have you learned?

1. **Jot down words or phrases to steal.**
2. **Write down ideas, characters, settings, plots you can use in your own writing.**
3. **Write down anything you have learned about the exam, punctuation, spelling.**
4. **Rewrite part of the answer to give it great grades.**

_____

_____

_____

_____

_____

_____

_____

_____

_____

_____

_____

<u>Response 6</u>

89 *percent of the population was wiped* out by the final war, just two centuries ago. Many believe the planet's destruction could now be *reset by the survivors **who had caused it so** much pain*. Some believe governments agreed to reduce the population. They claim **leaders treated people as mere statistics**. I no longer claim to know the truth.

Chemicals spread across our world. Now **science has leaped ahead** of all predictions. Space travel is a pastime money can buy. Money. These *days, everything depends* on money.

Rockets reflect and harness solar power to *fuel their shining flights*. Some believe the fuels are from the corpses **of the fallen**, but they have no proof.

Transport is now ridiculously exciting. We *fly in fast*, relaxing cars. But the special thrill comes in the gravity-free tube. Step inside a beam of light and you are transported a huge distance in an instant. You can travel from one side of Russia to the other in 89 minutes!

Naturally, this technological advance has transformed health and the discovery of species.

New creatures from land and sea are discovered weekly. Submersibles dive to great depths and thousands of species have been found every year for a century.

Our people have never been more healthy. Science has eliminated many faulty genes and terminal diseases. Killers from the past, like dementia, cancer and AIDs **have been tamed**, and now are rarely detected.

Yet each advance **brings a step backwards**. Zoos are filling with animals for our entertainment, when instead they should be protected. Doubling life expectancy has led to too many people.

I worry our world is ending.

This time we may face extinction ourselves.

I write this for a future reader. It is New Year's Day, in 2222. Don't repeat our mistakes.

May God be with you.

Eve

302 words

AO5 20

Original AO6 11

My Commentary

AO5

1. The student is trying to start each sentence with a different word.

2. The imagined future has a story behind it – both in the past, and what it will lead to in the future. This gives it a narrative drive.

3. The student uses vocabulary really precisely, nearly always choosing words which are really specific, rather than general. They feel exact.

4. There is no use of similes, but more frequent use of metaphors. Metaphors are usually more sophisticated than similes.

5. The student uses lots of emotive language to control our emotions.

6. It uses contrast a lot.

7. The student has introduced a character in order to give it an interesting structure – this allows them to turn the description into a letter of warning. It is very unlikely that this was planned. Simply putting the character into the writing has suddenly given the student this excellent ending. It is one of the reasons I recommend you always introduce a character. Can you remember the others?

8. Why isn't the writing yet inventive and compelling? Well, I feel it is still too short. And it is more of an explanation than a story or description. The idea that the rocket fuel is made from corpses feels odd, as it is not pursued – this makes it less convincing. Introducing zoos towards the end is also odd – it suggests this worse for society than using corpses for fuel.

Compelling, Convincing Communication   **22-24 marks**
   1. Extensive and ambitious vocabulary
   2. Sustained crafting of linguistic devices
   3. Varied and inventive use of structural features
   4. Fluently linked paragraphs

Convincing   **19–21 marks**
1-4 above, but not inventive and compelling

AO6

Level 3: Usually Imaginative and Usually Accurate   **9-12 marks**
   1. A range of punctuation is used, mostly accurate
   2. Uses a variety of sentence forms for effect
   3. Mostly uses Standard English appropriately
   4. Few mistakes in grammar
   5. Mostly accurate spelling, including complex and irregular words
   6. Increasingly sophisticated use of vocabulary

Response 7

2222 and life is reduced to agonies and destructive forces. Black cloud **envelops the sky**. The once beautiful *sky is now **the shroud of lost hopes and joys***. The cloud's thickness means the sun is *powerless to penetrate* it, and any **light is swallowed up by toxic airs**. The soils have boiled and cracked. The once green earth has died. The once great cities have died. All is agony and destruction. Parasites and diseases have spread across the land, above ground. Any person foolish enough to climb to the *surface would surely perish instantly, without protection*. The air would suck out their lungs, their *skin would blister and shed like a snake*, and their eyes grow *bloodshot and bulbous*.

Radiation released over a century ago **still preys on** every living thing, **like a starving predator**. **Radiation walks the land feeding on life**. Civilisations have been laid waste, and *desolation has destroyed* families and emptied cities.

And yet. Beneath the sickening ground is life. Humanity. Parents. Infants. A century of a new normality. The nuclear onslaught kept at *bay by giant bunkers* lined with *layers of lead* and steel. Mankind has grown pale skinned, hiding from the burning sun, exposed only to artificial lighting.

Every lake and river has *been boiled* from the surface. Only the sea is left. The salt filled sea. We stay hydrated one *salty sip* at a time. This is life for the human poor. And yet The *Paradise remains for the rich*.

The Paradise is its own world. Vibrant with the colours of nature. Saturated in oxygen. Disease free. And fresh water. Paradise for all who live there. But the cost is 500 million each.

279 words

AO5 22

Original AO6 12

My Commentary

AO5

1. Although there are a number of sentences starting with 'the', we can see that the student is experimenting with different ways of starting sentences.

2. The student is playing around with sentence lengths. Notice the short one word, curtailed sentences, to create a sense of drama, especially toward the end.

3.   Notice the sentences with several clauses in them, to build detail – follow the commas to find them.

4. Notice that the student keeps varying the length of sentences in nearly every paragraph.

5. Although the ending is rushed, we can see that the student has tried to build their whole answer around contrasts.

6. Repetition is also used frequently, especially to contrast the past with the present.

7. You will notice some similes and metaphors.

8. Alliteration and sibilance are often used to emphasise particular descriptions.

9. The student has thought really hard about their choice of verbs – reduce, penetrate, envelop, swallow, boil just in the opening few lines. Choosing the best verbs is the second easiest way to make your writing convincing and compelling.

10. If we had to sum up what compelling and convincing means it would be:

- starting sentences with different words,
- using brilliant verbs,
- varying the length of sentences,
- using the **big five**.
- Crafting an ending (an easy way is to refer back to the beginning for a circular structure).

Compelling, Convincing Communication   **22-24 marks**
1. Extensive and ambitious vocabulary
2. Sustained crafting of linguistic devices
3. Varied and inventive use of structural features
4. Fluently linked paragraphs

AO6

Level 3: Usually Imaginative and Usually Accurate   **9-12 marks**
1. A range of punctuation is used, mostly accurate
2. Uses a variety of sentence forms for effect
3. Mostly uses Standard English appropriately
4. Few mistakes in grammar
5. Mostly accurate spelling, including complex and irregular words
6. Increasingly sophisticated use of vocabulary

What have you learned?

1. **Jot down words or phrases to steal.**
2. **Write down ideas, characters, settings, plots you can use in your own writing.**
3. **Write down anything you have learned about the exam, punctuation, spelling.**
4. **Rewrite part of the answer to give it great grades.**

_____

_____

_____

_____

_____

_____

_____

_____

_____

_____

<u>**Response 8**</u>

<u>Journal: 27th of July E.D. 1221</u>

I wondered if it had been a joke, or *some sick satire to test* my faith. I never it imagined it would actually work.

I'd spent my life doing as my parents, and the Church told me. *Church, chores, family, faith*; I'd never done less than my best. Apart from my 13th birthday, three years ago, when I'd asked to dig in the orchard because I'd found some end-of-times metal and plastic, and my parents forbade me. It was against the Church, they said.

And so I passed by the undug orchard each day; I'd walk to schoolhouse where I learned to write with ink and a quill pen made *from finest goose feather*, which I sharpened with my own knife. By my fifteenth year Miss Peters had made me her assistant and I learned to teach the younglings how to read. But today will be different.

Today is my sixteenth birthday, 27th July E.D. (End of Days) 1221 and I've prepared a night time dig by moonlight. **Tonight I'll dig into the past**.

Ever since I was a youngling, my great grandmother told me the stories from her younghood. How the end-of-timers built cities **that scraped the clouds in the sky**, and how they *made metal wagons, some with impossible wings*. No one knows how these flew. She told me of buildings in her home town of Birm-in-Ham which were made of glass. People must have seemed **as though they were floating in the air**. They made *plastic* dolls and *parts* of wagons and bottles, and *strange shapes impossible* to understand. You know what farmers do when they *plough* some up: say the Lord's *Prayer* and give it to the *priest* for Sunday's bonfire. Even the younglings *find* plastic in the *fields* and give it to Reverend Matthias.

I spent my younghood wondering how the end-of-timers spoke to each other *across mountains and seas*. My great grandmother told me they used magical boxes, called Eye-Phoney, perhaps because they fooled the eye. When you looked at these wonders, my great grandmother said, you lost your soul. It was just like Adam and Eve and the apple. Indeed, the Eye-Phone was decorated with an apple. Yes, the end-of-timers made jokes about God.

In my ninth summer I asked mother, "Why did the end-of-timers forget about God?"

"When you get too clever, you think you are as clever as God. The end-of-timers, it is said, began to make plants which God had never planted, and animals which God had never made flesh," mother explained.

And yet they had lived in **cities which touched the sky**, and flew in metal wagons which crossed the sky, and spoke into magic boxes which took their words and *faces across the seas. What wonders* those people *were*.

My father *whipped* me with the horse reins when I first spoke about this *wonder*. I learned to stay silent. **But my mind would not be silenced**.

And so tonight I have my spade and trowel. This morning in the orchard I noticed a quarter inch of silver as I picked the fruit, and stamped it down.

<u>Journal: 28th July E.D. 1221</u>

It is past midnight. If you are reading this, it is because I am gone.

I dug up the silver metal. It is too slim to be called a box, but it *shimmers with silver* even after all *these centuries*. One side is perfect glass.

I've cleaned it, polished it, uncovered the blasphemous apple on its back. And then I pressed its edges to try to prise open a lid.

The glass lit up from within, and *strange diagrams **sprang** to life*. I touched one, and printed words appeared. "Face Id". And then a sound. A voice.

"Hello Eve," it said. "We have been waiting."

633 words

AO5 24

Original AO6 16

My Commentary

AO5

1. The student's story was set in the future, where trees no longer grow because of man's destruction of nature. It was 620 words long.

2. I've copied the length of each sentence, and the punctuation (though I changed one semi-colon to a colon). I've used similes and metaphors where they used them.

3. Notice that it is jam-packed with sibilance and alliteration.

4. The twist at the end of their story was that the narrator had found some old seeds and planted them, and a single tree had grown. The world's only tree. The examiner was so excited to read a story with an actual ending in which no one was killed that they gave it full marks.

5. It used humour, so the narrator had a pet dolphin and two pet monkeys. But these details undermined the world building – would a future in which we had destroyed all trees be a future in which we still had monkeys? Yet it still scored 100%.

6. The world I have created in this story is much more developed and convincing, but that is only because I have read more books. If you are interested, I stole this world from *The Second Sleep* by Robert Harris (interestingly my least favourite book of his because of its ending).

7. World building automatically makes your writing compelling and convincing, so long as everything fits together. It also allows you to make up words, like 'youngling', and 'end-of-timers' which everyone can understand, but feel special to that world.

8. Having a narrator makes starting each sentence with a different word more difficult. However, it does let you use a lot of repetition to create a kind of rhythm to their narrative.

9. Notice that the full mark examples are nearly always stories.

Compelling, Convincing Communication   **22-24 marks**
- Extensive and ambitious vocabulary
- Sustained crafting of linguistic devices
- Varied and inventive use of structural features
- Fluently linked paragraphs

AO6

Level 4: Imaginative and Accurate   **13-16 marks**
- Wide range of punctuation is used with a high level of accuracy
- Uses a full range of appropriate sentence forms for effect
- Uses Standard English consistently and appropriately
- No mistakes with grammar
- Very few mistakes in spelling, including ambitious vocabulary
- Extensive and ambitious use of vocabulary

What have you learned?

1. Jot down words or phrases to steal.
2. Write down ideas, characters, settings, plots you can use in your own writing.
3. Write down anything you have learned about the exam, punctuation, spelling.
4. Rewrite part of the answer to give it great grades.

_____

_____

_____

_____

_____

_____

_____

_____

_____

_____

_____

_____

_____

_____

_____

_____

_____

_____

_____

Final Full Mark Example

James was *finishing the fence* repairs when the messenger arrived. "It's for you, Mr Bond." James rolled his eyes. "It's Pond," he said, not for the first time. The messenger *unsealed a splendid scroll from his saddle* bag, *handed* it over, and rode away, *humming*.

Anxiously, James wiped his forearm on his *brow, and breathed deeply*. It was royal, obviously sealed with an official *ring with royal* insignia. Carefully, he walked to the porch, *cradling the scroll* as though it *contained* a dangerous spell.

"Amelia!" he summoned his wife, who *appeared to be baking apple pies* and scones again.

She staggered past, careful not to spill her load, her hands perfectly level. She glanced wide-eyed at the scroll. She forgot her baking. Shoving the *hot trays on the table*, she *snatched the scroll, gazed* at it, **like a *princess* with a mirror**. "It's from Charlotte," she announced excitedly, "we haven't seen each other in years. And we are to dine with her...tonight."

James's expression looked rather alarmed. "A bit late notice," he muttered nervously. The anxious couple held each other's gaze, both *apprehensive* and excited, then *propelled* themselves into exhilarated *preparation*.

Time *slowed,* *while they washed* off all evidence of the farm, and Amelia came forth, sporting her only intact dress and James trailed her in *his best Sunday shirt*. A carriage announced itself, its two *sleek,* white *horses tossing their tasselled* manes, and crunched to a stop at the gate. A splendid footman got down, opened the carriage, his immaculate silk uniform framed by the black veneer of the polished coach.

As they pulled away, James almost allowed a smile. This was better than Eyesore, their donkey; they felt **as though they were *cushioned by a cloud*, floating across** the muddy tracks. Time felt as though it had stopped (but actually two hours had passed) when the coach halted, and once more, a silk glove opened the carriage door. Amelia danced out, and they marvelled at what they saw.

They were surrounded by architecture, overwhelmed by *sculpted facades and soaring* columns. Perhaps it was too decorative to love, but to Amelia's mind, it was a perfect *spectacle. There stood a statue of Venus* in the *courtyard, hair cascading* down, in perfect, delicate marble, and Amelia, with her farmer's complexion and black hair, suddenly felt exposed, naked, and very, very inadequate. James, catching her eye, shared the feeling of awe with her.

Almost silently, the *great* oak *doors glided* open, and they *slowly stepped* through them; more *Greek gods and goddesses* on either *side seemed to salute their passage*, their blind painted eyes, realistically coloured, seemed to follow the red heat of their embarrassment.

"Amelia!" called a young woman, of the same age, as she glided towards Amelia and offered a cheek. Catherine, or Cat as she used to be known, clearly expected an air kiss, so she was alarmed when Amelia embraced her in a tight hug. Gently, to hide her embarrassment, Catherine slowly withdrew and smoothed her curls before taking in James.

"And you *must be Mr Pond! Meet my* husband Count Blofeld. I'm sure you both will find much in common."

A gentleman stepped out from behind her, strong, elegant and *perfectly proportioned* like the statues which had lined the entrance.

Amelia gasped at him. He was godlike. Though James was muscled from years of labour, she reluctantly noted his skin was cracked, his face browned and lined. James watched her blush, and he turned to Catherine, her *sky* blue *silk* gown *offset* by winking *emeralds*, and he was reminded of *summer meadows and birdsong*. An *ambiguous smile played on her perfect lips, as* she turned to Amelia.

"Now, what are you going to bake for us tonight?"

692 words

AO5 24

Original AO6 16

My Commentary

1. I really like this ending, where we are left wondering if they have only been invited so that they can cook, not as guests at all.

2. This will work both as a description and a story, because the characters and setting are described so well.

3. This is much better than writing a description, because of course it is like real writing you meet in a book.

4. Like all good writing, everything is based on contrasts.

5. The ending was really easy to plan. The student's ending was not as well crafted, it was 'It was going to be a long night', a hint of the troubles to come, which the reader could fill in. Or, this could equally be the first chapter of a book, and so the next chapter would try to explore the conflict further.

6. Another way of thinking about the ending is, "how can I end it with a contrast to what the characters are expecting?" Contrast solves most problems in writing.

7. It is also worth understanding your setting. Creating a different world (world building) is a really easy way to take control of your writing and make it different to other students in the exam. The setting will allow you to predict the sort of vocabulary that you will be able to use.

8. For example, pick a fairy tale type setting. Think of Cinderella, etc. write down 5 great pieces of vocabulary to describe each of these:

- Jewellery
- A rich man's clothes. Then a farmer's.
- A rich woman's clothes. Then a farmer's wife.
- A farm house.
- A mansion or palace.
- A statue, or art.
- A horse.
- A carriage.
- Anything else you associate with this genre.

9. It will be incredibly easy to make any image, or any narrative title, fit a fairy tale setting. For example, a picture of a passenger on a bus could simply begin:

- "She looked out at the dreary streets, feeling trapped by her stifling commute and turned her gaze inwards, to her weary life. Then, with a feeling like hope, she opened her book..."

- "She gazed out of the bus at the mad hustle and bustle of twenty first century living, at neon dazzled streets and pedestrians glued to the dopamine fix of their screens and longed for a simpler time. She opened her book."

- "Work was awful. The weather was awful. The economy was awful. But none of this mattered to Amelia, because the latest novel by her favourite author was sitting on her lap. She turned the page."

- "The bus journey held no joys for Amelia. She let the outside world disappear, and entered a richer landscape in her mind..."

- "Nigella thought she had seen everything Fairy Folk would ever see until she was nearly splatted on the windscreen of the 159 bus from Kilburn. How in fairy-hell, she thought, had a human bus jumped through the space-time-fairy-continuum?"

10. Many of you will have other worlds you are deeply familiar with which would work just as well. You might prepare a list of vocabulary for your world. Perhaps:

- You grew up in another country.
- You love a particular genre of book – you can certainly set it in Hogwarts, etc.
- You love a particular film franchise – you can make it a spy story, or set in Tony Stark's/ Iron Man's home, or take two of the characters from Friends, or go on a mission in Call of Duty or Fortnite. Anything which gives you a world you can instantly picture and therefore bring to life.
- If you prepare your vocabulary in advance, your writing will always be interesting, and you will have more thinking time available to crafting your writing.

11. I also find it helps to be playful in my choice of name. You will have spotted James Bond (notice you need to change an obvious name. Whatever you do, don't call them Bob). Changing it to Pond gave me Amelia's name – Amelia Pond was one of Doctor Who's assistants. Blofeld is a James Bond villain. Catherine is an entitled and very bitchy ex-girlfriend of the detective, Strike, in J.K. Rowling's adult novels.

The reader doesn't have to spot any of this. But using characters like this, on the spur of the moment, means that I don't have to think hard and slowly – I can already picture them – so my writing is both quicker and more creative.

So, steal ideas from the books you read.

Compelling, Convincing Communication   **22-24 marks**
- Extensive and ambitious vocabulary
- Sustained crafting of linguistic devices
- Varied and inventive use of structural features

- Fluently linked paragraphs

AO6

Level 4: Imaginative and Accurate   **13-16 marks**
- Wide range of punctuation is used with a high level of accuracy
- Uses a full range of appropriate sentence forms for effect
- Uses Standard English consistently and appropriately
- No mistakes with grammar
- Very few mistakes in spelling, including ambitious vocabulary
- Extensive and ambitious use of vocabulary

What have you learned?

1. Jot down words or phrases to steal.
2. Write down ideas, characters, settings, plots you can use in your own writing.
3. Write down anything you have learned about the exam, punctuation, spelling.
4. Rewrite part of the answer to give it great grades.

_____

_____

_____

_____

_____

_____

_____

_____

_____

_____

_____

_____

_____

_____

_____

_____

_____

_____

_____

_____

_____

Top Vocabulary Used at Grades 8 and 9 (345 words)

abundance	billboards	crystalline	fragrance	lace	peered	scorched
abyss	blackened	dazzling	frail	laughed	penetrated	scraping
absorb	blanketed	debris	frock	launching	perilous	screeching
accepting	blazing	decay	fulfilled	leaped	perish	sedentary
abandoned	bleak	delinquent	fumes	lifeless	permeating	settle
abrupt	bless	demise	furiously	limb	petrified	shade
acquainted	blinding	derelict	gaping	liquid	pierced	shadow
ancient	blurry	desolate	gargantuan	loudly	pile	shallow
ago	brambles	dignity	garment	luscious	pillars	shame
aggressively	breath-taking	dim	gleaming	magical	pinnacle	sharply
aloud	breaths	diamante	glide	magnificent	pleading	shelter
although	brew	disobediently	glimpse	mahogany	pleasant	shimmering
amongst	brightness	distant	glistening	majestic	plumes	shoved
anxiously	brutal	distorted	gloom	mansion	pooled	shrapnel
apart	brute	distressed	gloomily	masked	pounded	shrieks
apparently	bulging	dreary	glorious	matted	poured	shrouding
approach	bustling	drenched	glowing	measly	presence	sighed
arose	caged	eagerness	gold-tinted	measure	pressure	silhouette
arrival	cancer	eerily	golden	meddling	prominent	silver
arrogant	cannibalistic	elaborately	golems	memories	protruded	slab
ashamed	capture	elegant	gravity	merciless	proud	slammed
assault	carriages	embarrassment	greeted	merely	pummelling	sleek
assume	carved	emitted	grime	merrily	pungent	slender
atmosphere	cascading	emanating	grimly	midst	putrid	slumped
attack	casing	encircle	habitual	mimicking	puzzled	smooth
attempt	cast	enriched	harm	miserable	radiated	snapped
attraction	casual	entice	harsh	mixture	reassuring	snatching
aura	chaos	envelope	hoarsely	modesty	rebelliously	soaked
available	chapter	eradicate	howling	moisture	relentless	sobbed
awaited	charm	eroding	hues	monstrous	remains	soot
awe	cheerful	erratically	humanity	neon	reminisced	sorrowful
barrages	chirping	etched	hung	nervously	remorse	soulless
barriers	clambered	eternal	hurling	never-ending	renowned	sparring
base	clanking	evident	hurtled	nostalgia	resigned	sparkled
bashed	clung	exposed	hushed	oblivious	respectably	spectacle
battle	cluster	expressive	illuminating	observe	restrain	spilled
battlefield	clutching	extended	immediately	obsessively	revealed	spindly
beaten	coursed	exterior	immersed	offensively	riddled	spirited
beautifully	collapse	fascinated	impatiently	onslaught	ridges	splashed
became	collided	ferociously	impenetrable	optimism	rippling	spotless
before	colossal	fiddling	impolite	overgrown	risen	spraying
behind	comfort	fidget	inconclusive	overwhelming	risk	spreading
believing	complacent	fiery	inconsistent	pale	roams	spun
belonging	concave	floral	inhaling	pallid	ruin	squelching
beloved	concealed	foaming	intense	panic-stricken	rumbled	stark
below	courtyard	forehead	intervals	paradise	ruthless	stench
beneath	creature	forged	jolt	parasites	sandy	wading
benefit	crevice	foundation	journey	patiently	scenic	wails
besides	crusty	fragile	joy	peeked	scent	warmth
						warped

How to Use This List

Senses

Pick out a range of vocabulary dealing with sounds. Pick a noisy scene to describe with the words. Then pick a calm scene to describe soft sounds.

Do the same with texture and touch. Then with smells. Finally, with taste.

Character

Pick vocabulary to describe a heroic character we are supposed to admire. Do the same for a villain. Write both descriptions.

Put both characters at the beginning of a story, and write about them as part of the same story.

Pick vocabulary to describe an old character. Then a young one. Write about them as above.

Atmosphere, Mood, Tone

Think of a scene where a character is happy, joyful, at peace. Pick vocabulary which will help you write that scene, and write it.

Think of a scene where the character is sad, angry, anxious. Pick vocabulary to write that scene.

Combine both of the above with writing about your characters (which means that your description will be the same as a real writer, rather than just to prove you are describing).

Setting

There are typical setting which can occur in most exam question and stories. Pick vocabulary to write about each of these:

1. The countryside
2. A city
3. The past – the sort of setting you would get in a fairy-tale
4. The future – the sort of setting Earth might be in 200 years
5. A place you would like to be
6. A place you would like to avoid

These 6 will cover any exam question you will ever get.

Simile, Metaphor, Personification

Find nouns which are not similar. For example billboards and battlefield. Write about one, using the other as a comparison.

Do the same, but find verbs from the list which you can add. For example, how can the billboard cascade or bustle or ripple etc.

This will be difficult, but because it is difficult, you will come up with creative solutions which lead to great writing.

Parts of Speech

Find 10 great verbs. Use these to write about a character.

Do the same to write about an animal.

Now find 10 to write about a robot or a machine, or both.

Do the same 3 tasks with adjectives.

Soundscape

Find 10 words which sound harsh because of their consonants. Write a scene with a harsh atmosphere.

Find 10 words with soft sounds, because of the softness of the vowels and consonants. Write a scene with peaceful atmosphere.

Choose words from the alphabetic list. Write a scene in which you use groups of words beginning with each letter. (Although you can warm up writing sentences with too much alliteration, edit them so that they gradually feel more natural).

Artificial Difficulties

- Pick a word from several lists at random (say 15). Use each word in a scene.
- Pick a specific word from several list (e.g. the sixth word in the list). Use each word in a scene.
- Write a 25-50 word sentence using as many of the words as you can.
- Pick words at random. Use only one per sentence.
- Pick words at random. Use at least three per sentence. (Or increase this number).
- Find all the adverbs, or 15 adjectives, or 20 verbs and try to use all in the list to write a scene.
- Do the same with colours

Creating artificial rules like this will force you to be much more creative.

If you've found this guide useful, please give it a review on Amazon. It will help me reach more students to show them how to get top grades. And it will help me spend more time making videos so students can learn these skills for free.

Printed in Great Britain
by Amazon